D1281921

EVANGELISM EXPLOSION

D. JAMES KENNEDY

FOREWORD BY BILLY GRAHAM

TYNDALE HOUSE PUBLISHERS
Wheaton, Illinois

Coverdale House Publishers, London and Eastbourne, England

Eighteenth printing, November 1976
360,000 copies in print

Library of Congress Catalog Card No. 71-116480
ISBN 8423-0780-X
Copyright © 1970 D. James Kennedy
Printed in U.S.A.

This book
is affectionately dedicated
to the hundreds of laymen and laywomen
of the Coral Ridge Presbyterian Church
who have faithfully over the years put into practice
the principles and methods of this program.

9

CONTENTS

THE AUTHOR

Dr. D. James Kennedy was born in Augusta, Georgia, reared in Chicago and has spent most of his life in Florida. He received his B.A. Degree from the University of Tampa and his B.D. Cum Laude from Columbia Theological Seminary, and his Master of Theology, Summa Cum Laude, from the Chicago Graduate School of Theology. He received the Doctor of Divinity Degree from Trinity College and Trinity Evangelical Divinity School. For the last several summers he has been working toward the Ph.D. Degree in the External Program of the University of London.

Dr. Kennedy has lectured and taught in a number of seminaries and colleges and the General Assemblies of a number of denominations. He has spoken to over 14,000 ministers and seminary students on the subject of lay evangelism. He is a regular member of the faculty of the Billy Graham Schools of Evangelism.

THE RESULTS OF THIS PROGRAM

Almost 300 people are engaged in a weekly program of lay evangelism in the Coral Ridge Presbyterian Church in Fort Lauderdale, Florida. Some of the tangible results of this program are seen in the following facts. For four years the church has been the fastest growing church in the Presbyterian Church in the United States. In nine years the church has grown from nothing to over 2,000 members, from one minister to five and to a peak attendance of over 2,850 in four morning services. In stewardship the church has grown from home mission support to a budget of over $750,000. In the past year alone some ten families have decided to go into full-time Christian service.

FOREWORD

by Billy Graham

The Reverend Dr. D. James Kennedy is minister of the Coral Ridge Presbyterian Church of Fort Lauderdale, Florida, and I have known him for several years and followed his ministry closely. So enthusiastic have I become over his program for evangelizing a parish that I have asked him to come regularly and address our Crusade School of Evangelism, where he has been before many thousands of theological students, ordinands, young clergy and other Christian workers.

Dr. Kennedy was not always a preacher. Indeed, he was a dancing instructor, par excellence, with the Arthur Murray Dancing School and rapidly rising into prominence in that profession. Then one day his clock radio brought him a disturbing question from Dr. Donald Gray Barnhouse, the Philadelphia preacher, concerning where he would spend his eternal destiny. He could turn off his radio, but he could not turn off the eternal implication of this all-important question. The result was a revolutionary conversion. He subjected himself to the disciplines of being trained for and ordained into the ministry.

Christianity Today magazine correctly describes his congregation as the fastest growing in the Presbyterian Church in the U.S. In nine years it has grown from none to more than two thousand members and this at a time when churches everywhere are complaining of dwindling memberships. There are doubtless a number of reasons for this phenomenal growth but I would like to cite two. The first is the unwavering devotion of Dr. Kennedy, as a man, to Jesus Christ his Lord, a devotion that counts no sacrifice too great, no cost too high to pay to give Jesus Christ his best. The second is the fact that Pastor Kennedy has recaptured the biblical concept that the Church's primary task is "every-member evangelism." The Church, having come to Christ, is to go for Christ. In this book, Dr. Kennedy outlines how a whole congregation can be motivated and mobilized to perform this task of evangelism. The pastor himself must provide the example and leadership in this task. He chooses trainees and in four months of engaging them an evening a week, trains them in the science and art of house-to-house evangelism. He teaches them the course. He goes with them and demonstrates how it is done. Then the trainees graduate into trainers and, in turn, train others. In the words of a Canadian pastor who saw 103 members added to his church in the first eight months of effecting this program, this plan of Dr. Kennedy's is "the most revolutionary technique for personal evangelism to mobilize the sleeping giant of our laity to be discovered in the twentieth century."

Unworthy as I may feel at times, it has been my privilege for 20 years to see many of the world's largest stadiums crowded to hear the claims of Christ presented from the Bible. Equally important in New Testament evangelism, however, is this basic principle of one-to-one evangelism.

PREFACE

There is something new in the life of the Christan Church today! It is the "Evangelism Explosion."

In recent years we have heard much about the "population explosion"—the burgeoning of masses of people at rates hitherto undreamed of. The population has been increasing at a far greater rate than the church. The reason for this is simple. While the world has been multiplying we have been making "additions to the church." It is patently obvious that if the church is adding while the world is multiplying there is no hope of our ever catching up.

The only answer to this dilemma, humanly speaking, is "spiritual multiplication." This involves the laity. In fact, it involves everyone who names the name of Christ.

The Evangelism Explosion is God's answer to the population explosion. Thousands of laymen and ministers, trained and equipped to graciously present the Gospel of Christ, provide the fissionable material. The Holy Spirit working through the Gospel, which is the **dunameis** or "dynamite" of God, provides the explosive power, and the result is not chaos but the creation of a vast host of new Christians who are in turn being trained to carry on this spiritual chain reaction.

At the World Consultation on Mobilization Saturation Evangelism held in Switzerland in mid-1969, it was noted that the decade of the Sixties had been the decade of the emerging laymen in the church. About the year 1960 a number of different groups and movements arose spontaneously in various parts of the world, all having the same vision: the mobilizing and equipping of the vast lay army of the church to do the work of ministry. It seems that after centuries of a clergy-oriented ministry the Holy Spirit is finally breaking through our man-made molds to create the type of church that He meant should exist from the beginning, and which did exist for the first three centuries of this era of our Lord.

That this is the movement of the Spirit of God in our time is further evidenced by the tremendous eagerness with which thousands of ministers are responding to the opportunities and potentiality of lay multiplication evangelism.

Laymen can not only be trained to witness but they can be trained to train others to witness and thus multiply their labors. It has been well said, "He is best employed who is involved in multipling the workers."

The results of such a lay evangelism program in our own church have been so astonishing that they would appear unbelievable to those who do not understand the spiritual power engendered by such a ministry. We are awed and humbled as we become almost observers to the mighty works of God, and we know that this is His doing and it is marvelous in our eyes.

The aim of this book is to help other churches, pastors, and laymen to learn better how to do person-to-person evangelism and also how to train others to do the same.* This book is designed as a textbook to be used in class sessions of an evangelistic program, as well as to be studied at home. Portions of the book should be assigned for study each week at home, and then recitation in class periods by dividing into twos is encouraged. The emphasis is on simply learning to tell the Gospel in a positive and gracious manner. A thorough approach to the Gospel is needed. We suggest that you learn the skeletal framework of the Outline first and then gradually add the flesh and muscles of illustrations and Scripture until you have developed a presentation which you "own" and which you can use on any occasion, whether you have three minutes or two hours to discuss the Gospel.

I would like here to express my sincere gratitude to the following publishers for their kind permission to use quotes from some of their published works: Presbyterian Church in the U. S., for quotes from "Worship and Work of the Congregation" and "Workable Plan of Assimilation"; Wm. B. Eerdmans Publishing Co., " New Testament Follow-Up"; Harper and Row, "Effective Evangelism"; and Lockman Foundation, "Follow-Up Made Easy."

Also I would like to acknowledge my gratitude to the many others now long forgotten and untraceable who nevertheless have been the source of many of the thoughts and illustrations in this book. In addition I would like to express my thanks to the Rev. Kennedy Smartt who patiently took me with him on home visitation and instructed me in the fine art of personal evangelism.

I would also like to express my appreciation and acknowledge my indebtedness to the many who have helped to make this book a reality. I would like to thank the Rev. Harry Miller who first gathered all our material together into notebook form; the Rev. Simeon Fulcher, our Minister to Youth, for his sections on Youth Evangelism and illustrations; the Rev. Archie Parrish, our Minister of Evangelism, for his Bibliography and for his work with the Rev. Ross Bair on Follow-up; Mr. James Carlson for the Follow-up Charts; to the dedicated group of men and women in our church who put this together as a notebook over and over again through the years for use in our church and clinics; to my personal secretary, Mrs. Mary Anne Bunker, for her constant assistance; and a most special word of appreciation and thanks to Mrs. Ruth Rohm, our publications secretary, for her faithful labors in typing, retyping, and editing the work.

D. James Kennedy

Fort Lauderdale, Florida
1970

TRAINING LAYMEN FOR EVANGELISM

A. Surveying the Program

This is not theory, but fact! These are not the idle speculations of the ivory tower but the tested results of hard experience. First in the congregation of the Coral Ridge Presbyterian Church of Fort Lauderdale, Florida, and then in hundreds of other churches, these principles and procedures have brought new life and vitality and have resulted in the conversion of thousands of people.

Readily transferable techniques

This program of training laymen for the task of evangelism grew out of the specific problems and opportunities faced by our congregation. Yet the program contains readily transferable techniques which have been used by other congregations. We believe that the principles contained in the program represent some of the basic principles of the New Testament concerning the matter of evangelism, though by no means does this program exhaust all of the biblical teaching and possibilities of evangelism. This is a program of personal lay evangelism and does not begin to encompass many of the other sound and biblical methods of evangelism, such as mass evangelism, pulpit evangelism, etc.

Realizing that laymen are the most strategic and also the most unused key to the evangelization of the world, we have endeavored to build a program which will motivate, recruit, and train men and women to do the job of evangelism——and then

Laymen——the strategic key

1

keep them doing it! This, of course, is not an easy task, as most pastors can testify. And yet it would seem that the basic principles of New Testament evangelism require that this mobilization of the laity take place. Let us look at some of these principles.

B. Examining the Principles

Every Christian a witness

Christ's first instructions to His new followers in the first chapter of Mark were, "Come ye after Me, and I will make you to become fishers of men." His last instructions on this earth to His disciples were, "But ye shall receive power, after that the Holy Ghost is come upon you: and ye shall be witnesses unto Me both in Jerusalem, and in all Judaea, and in Samaria, and unto the uttermost part of the earth." Christ thus began and ended His ministry with the command to be witnesses and fishers of men! This thrust of His teaching is summed up in the Great Commission where Jesus commands His followers to go into all of the world and preach the Gospel to every creature. **The first and most obvious principle, then, is that the Church is a body under orders by Christ to share the Gospel with the whole world.** But the question then arises, How is this to be done and by whom?

The wiles of Satan

The Apostle Paul said that we are not ignorant of the wiles of the devil. But I wonder how true that is today? I wonder how many times we have been deceived by him? I am sure it has been often. What is the greatest strategic victory that Satan has ever achieved? What would you suppose it to be? The most signal victory for Satan would obviously be the worst defeat for the Church. What might it be?

Satan's greatest victory

Surely a number of his devious stratagems leap to mind. I would like to suggest one thing which, in my opinion, is his greatest victory. Let me present it to you in the way of an analogy. Suppose that in our modern, secular world, the center

2

for propaganda in Moscow dreamed up a new idea. They polished it very carefully and then began to spread it abroad. It appears first of all in some avant-garde publications, coming to surface in magazine and newspaper articles. Perhaps a play would be made out of it, and then a motion picture, and finally a television production. Groups would be formed to push the movement, protests would be made, and finally the idea prevails and is accepted by the American people, almost unanimously. What is the idea? It is this: that wars are very dangerous, complicated operations and ordinary persons could get hurt needlessly, therefore they should go home and let the generals and admirals fight wars. I don't think there is any doubt in our minds as to what would be the outcome of the cold—or not so cold—war in which we are engaged.

Right away we say, "That is ridiculous! Such a ludicrous idea could never be put over on any people." Yet in the Church this, in essence, is exactly what Satan has done! I am certain that for the vast majority of Christian church members the idea has firmly taken root in their minds that it is primarily the task of the minister to fight the battles of Christ—especially for the souls of men. In the minds of most, the work of evangelism is the work of professionally trained men. "After all," they say, "I'm just a butcher, or baker or candlestick maker, and what do I know about theology? I've never been to seminary; leave it to the trained ecclesiastical generals!" This I believe has been the greatest tragedy that has befallen the Church of Jesus Christ. Its results are so far reaching, so vast in scope, that we have little concept of what damage has been done.

But it wasn't this way in the early Church! Examine again that passage in Acts 8:4 where it says, "All they that were scattered abroad went everywhere preaching the Word." That is a great text to preach. But some people might say, "Well, just a minute, preacher, not so fast. You have

**Let the generals
fight the war**

The early Church

3

turned that corner a little too rapidly. You see, the people that went everywhere spreading the Word and preaching the Word were the apostles. You remember, Jesus chose these Twelve and they were trained, and they went out and spread the Word.''

Everyone evangelizing!

Well, we all know that a standard exegetical axiom is, "A text without a context is a pretext," and this has been a pretext long enough for letting ecclesiastical George do it! The significant context of that verse is found in Acts 8:1 where we read that "they were all scattered abroad **except the apostles.**" And (Acts 8:4) "they that were scattered abroad went everywhere preaching the Word." The word translated "preaching the Word is the Greek word ευαγγελίζομαι which means "evangelizing." That is, everybody **except the apostles** went everywhere evangelizing! Now we know that the apostles did their share and more than that. But the point that the inspired writer is emphasizing here is that everyone besides the apostles also went and evangelized.

Results of lay evangelism

This is how the Church of Jesus Christ in 300 years accomplished the most amazing results. The whole pagan Roman Empire was undercut and overthrown by the power of the Gospel of Christ which, on the lips of Christ-conquered disciples, crossed seas and deserts, pierced the darkest jungles, seeped into every city and town, and finally into the senate and the very palace of Rome itself—until a Christian caesar was placed upon the throne. How? Because everyone was preaching the Word. The Christian Church was burgeoning with such rapidity that by the middle of the second century one of the great apologists could say, "We are everywhere. We are in your towns and in your cities; we are in your country; we are in your army and navy; we are in your palaces; we are in the senate; we are more numerous than anyone." Constantine knew very well (whether or not he was truly converted I will leave for the historians) that he had no chance

4

of unifying the Roman Empire or holding power in that empire without the help of the Christians.

By A.D. 300 the Church had shown such tremendous strength and virility, and was spreading so swiftly, that it appeared the entire civilized world could be evangelized by A.D. 500. But something happened. You remember. Emperor Constantine, supposing to do a favor to the church, by fiat decree, declared the whole Roman Empire to be Christian. Thus millions of barbarians flooded into the church, bringing with them all of the pagan superstitions and heresies. They didn't even know the Gospel. They had never experienced its transforming power and, of course, they could not go out and tell others about it. So, little by little, the idea arose that there was a division between the clergy and the laity, and that this task of evangelism was the job of the professionally trained individuals. So they decided to let ecclesiastical George do it. The Dark Ages followed! With only a few bright spots in the history of the church since that time, this deplorable condition has continued down to our day.

So successful has Satan been with this stratagem that it has been estimated that probably 95 percent of our church members have never led anyone to Christ. Thus the army of Christ has been more than decimated and the response from the pew has been, "Let clerical George do it." I am thankful that today there is an obvious trend in the opposite direction, as more and more laymen and churches are realizing and accepting their responsibility to witness.

The second important principle, then, is that laymen as well as ministers must be trained to evangelize. Over 99 percent of the church is made up of laymen. If they are A.W.O.L. there is little doubt that the battle will be lost.

If the laity has been deceived, I think it is equally true that the ministers have also been deceived

Clergy—laity split

Let clerical George do it

Importance of laymen

Purpose of ministers

5

by the subtlety of Satan concerning the basic purpose of their ministry. In the fourth chapter of Ephesians we read that Christ has given to the Church "some, apostles; and some, prophets; and some, evangelists; and some, pastors and teachers; for the perfecting of the saints, for the work of the ministry, for the edifying of the body of Christ." This is the way it reads in the King James translation. This, however, is not a very accurate rendering of the Greek text. Instead of the preposition "for" being repeated three times, the Greek says "πρoσ," "εισ," "εισ" which would be better rendered: "for," "unto," "unto." A more literal translation, then, would be that Christ has given pastors and teachers to the Church "for the equipping of the saints unto the work of ministry, unto the upbuilding of the body of Christ."

Revolutionary concept

Such a concept, once grasped, would completely revolutionize many ministries. A basic criterion for determining the successfulness of a pastorate would then become: "How many saints have I equipped to do the work of ministry?" **The third principle, then, that we need to grasp as ministers is to see ourselves not as the star performer or virtuoso but rather as the coach of a well-trained and well-coordinated team.**

We have seen what needs to be done and by whom; now let us ask: How are we going to get them to do it?

Missing key

There have been hundreds of thousands of messages preached on the responsibility of Christians to witness, and yet there is a striking absence of any formidable army of lay witnesses. Something, therefore, must be missing. This brings us to **our fourth important principle,** namely: **"Evangelism is more caught than taught."** This oft-repeated cliché rather accurately describes what is missing in most attempts at teaching laymen to evangelize and also fairly well describes the method that Christ used to teach His followers. I have asked thousands of ministers how many of them have preached sermons on the need to witness and have taught classes on this subject. Most of them have raised their hand, but when I have asked how many of them make a habit of taking their people with them when they go out to evangelize, only three or four percent will usually respond. I questioned a group of ministers, missionaries and teachers and found that only one and one-half percent of their members were regularly engaged in leading people to Christ, and only three of these people took their laymen with them when they went to evangelize. The average person can no more learn to evangelize in a classroom than he can learn to fly an airplane in the living room. The missing link of modern evangelistic training, which was so thoroughly provided by Christ, is "on-the-job" training.

The fifth principle of this program is that it is more important to train a soul-winner than to win a soul. Spiritual multiplication will not take place unless converts are turned into evangelists, disciples into disciplers. Since about 95 percent of converts never win anyone to Christ because they are not equipped thereunto, it is obvious that training a person to evangelize effectively will be more fruitful than merely winning someone to Christ. The Lord Jesus did not say to go and make converts but to go and make disciples. It is because winning a person to Christ is so important that training someone to win 10 or 100 people to Christ is so much more important. One of the wonderful parts of this program is that these two task are combined and people are trained to evangelize by observing as others are being evangelized. Thus one is not done to the exclusion of the other.

These are the basic principles that we feel need to be understood and accepted if a church is to have an effective program of evangelism.

On-the-job training

C. Reviewing the History

Fear of witnessing

This program grew out of the experiences I had in starting the Coral Ridge church, which was a home mission project, now nine years old. I came directly to this work from seminary and though I preached evangelistically and I had taken all the courses offered at seminary on evangelism and read many books besides, I found that the sophisticated people of Fort Lauderdale did not respond to my message from the pulpit. I was totally lacking in both confidence and know-how as far as confronting individuals face to face with the Gospel. After eight or ten months of my preaching, the congregation had gone from 45 to 17, and I was a most discouraged young minister. About that time I was invited to Decatur, Georgia, to preach ten days of evangelistic services. Happy to get away for a while from my Fort Lauderdale fiasco, I accepted the invitation.

Life-changing experience

When I arrived the pastor told me that I would be preaching each night, but more importantly, he said, we would be visiting in the homes each day—morning, noon and night—to present the Gospel to people individually. I was petrified for I knew I had no ability whatsoever to do this. However, the next morning we went out. After about a half hour of my stumbling attempts at evangelism, the pastor took over the conversation and in about 15 or 20 minutes led the man to Christ. I was astonished but did not realize even then the impact that this was to have on my life. For ten days I watched this pastor lead one person after another to Christ for a total of 54 individuals during those ten days. I went back to Fort Lauderdale a new man, and I began to do just what I had seen done. People responded. Soon dozens, scores, and then hundreds accepted Christ. The principle of "on-the-job" training had been applied to my life, and had produced its results.

Failure of classes

I then realized that there was a definite limit to

8

the number of people that I myself could see, and that I ought to train others to do the same thing. What I then foolishly did is the same thing that thousands of others no doubt have done: I organized a class on witnessing. I gave them six lessons and sent them out. They all went home terrified! I waited a few months and tried again. This time I gave them 12 lessons—again no success. A few more months and another series, more elaborate, more complex; 15 weeks—again no results. I do not know of one single adult that was brought to Christ by one of these laymen as a result of these witnessing classes.

Finally it struck me like a bolt of lightning—I had taken classes for three years and had not learned how to witness. It was not until someone who knew how had taken me out into people's homes that I finally got the confidence to do it myself. Thus I began the program which has continued for the past eight years. It began by my taking out one individual until he had confidence to witness to others, and then another, and another. And so it has grown. After the people are trained, they in turn can train others.

The missing link

D. Motivating the Christians

Often when an evangelism program is envisioned, a pastor will begin by preaching on the subject and then inviting everybody who is willing to take part to come on a specified night to begin the program. This is the way we tried at first to motivate people and recruit them, but we found it was not very successful. The basic motivation will no doubt begin from the pulpit with sermons on the responsibility, privilege, and necessity for witnessing for Christ. The great texts already mentioned, and others, should certainly be preached with clarity and forcefulness. However, our experience teaches us that the actual recruiting should not be done from the pulpit, but rather should be done on a person-to-person basis, first by the pastor and then by the trained laymen.

Problems of mass recruitment

9

E. Recruiting the Workers

Individual invitation

When Christ called His apostles, He first prayed all night and then called them specifically by name. Now an apostle ($\alpha\pi\sigma\sigma\tau\lambda\sigma s$) was one sent forth with a commission. The term has both a narrow and a wider meaning. In its narrow sense it refers only to the twelve apostles whom Christ first called. In its broader sense it refers to every Christian who has been sent forth by Christ with a Great Commission. We would therefore recommend that after much prayer the minister select several people whom he would like to take with him to learn how to evangelize. (I might add at this point that we have changed from going out by twos to going out by threes. The reason for this was that it solved the problem of what to do about women in a program of this sort. To send out two women at night in a modern city can be quite dangerous; to send out one woman with somebody else's husband can be dangerous in a different way. To send out **only** husbands and wives defeats the purpose of multiplication.)

Three-by-three

Report-back sessions

We have selected Wednesday morning from 9 to 12 and Thursday evening from 7:15 to 10:30 as our time of visitation. In each case we have a report-back meeting which I feel is quite important to prevent discouragement. On Wednesday noon we have lunch together; we provide coffee and the people bring a bag lunch. On Thursday night we provide Sanka and doughnuts. At these times we hear the reports of the work of the day. These report sessions help reduce drop-outs due to discouragement, as evangelists have an opportunity to have their spirits lifted by returning to hear others whom God has blessed that night or morning.

Not three men

I would suggest that the pastor begin by selecting two people for Wednesday morning and two others for Thursday night. As long as we do not have three men together, which seems a bit heavy, we have not found that the three indi-

10

viduals constitute much of a problem. The reason for going out by threes was that it solved the problem of what to do with women in the program. Someone might say, "But doesn't the Bible tell us that we should go out two-by-two? Well, let us take a closer look at that passage. There is no doubt that Christ sent out the Seventy, two-by-two. But the question arises, "Whom did He send out?" I believe there is little doubt that He sent out 70 men. If, however, He had had 35 men and 35 women, what would He have done then? This, of course, was not feasible in that day. Today it is. In our time, to send out two women into a modern metropolis at night is exceedingly dangerous. To send out a woman with somebody else's husband is also dangerous, but three is still a crowd under any circumstances. Sending them out by threes has the double advantage of including women in the program and also doubling the speed of training. Someone might ask, "Can't you send out a husband and wife together?" Yes, you can, but this is a dead-end street, for the whole purpose of this program is to continually expand the number of people trained and you cannot do this without dividing the husband and wife team.

We have two training programs a year, the first beginning early in October and running about four and a half months until the middle of February. At this time we hold our clinic for ministers, which lasts five days. Then we begin our next training class which runs till the beginning of summer. All of these details will vary according to local customs and circumstances.

Length of training

I did not want to begin a program in this small way with only one or two individuals, but wanted rather to train a whole class of evangelists at one time. The result was that I ended up with none. However, if you begin with a few, you can grow in not too much time into a large body of witnesses. At the end of the four and a half month training program, each of these four trained indi-

Rapid multiplication

viduals would recruit two more workers and the minister also would recruit four more. Now there would be the original four plus their eight, making twelve, plus the minister's new four, making sixteen, plus the minister, or a total of seventeen. After the next class the sixteen laymen would get thirty-two more, making forty-eight, plus the minister's four, which makes fifty-two, plus the minister, making fifty-three. And soon it could grow to a hundred, two hundred, etc.

Recruitment banquets

The people are recruited by personal visits at which time the program is explained by the trained individual in detail and then they are invited to a dinner which will consist of a greater explanation of the goals and principles and reasons for the program, plus testimonies of what has been accomplished. Then they are asked to commit themselves to the entire four and a half month training program or else not to start. Paul said, "I am afraid of you, lest I have bestowed on you labor in vain."

F. Training the Evangelists
Our program consists of **three types of training.**

1. Class instruction

Types of training

These classes, lasting about a half hour each, are held one a week on the day the people come to the church for visitation. They meet together for class instruction for a half hour and then go out into the field. During this class instruction there is a brief lecture on the topic of the week, assignments are given for study during the following week, and the class is divided into twos where they practice what has been learned during the previous week.

2. Homework assignments

This detailed workbook contains instructions on how to present the Gospel logically and interestingly. Assignments are given each week, consisting of portions of the Gospel presentation to be learned. These are checked and recited each week at the class.

3. On-the-job training
   The third and most important part of the training is "on-the-job." Here each trainee goes out with a trained individual and listens as this trained person endeavors to lead someone to Christ. **This is the vital, almost indispensable, element of training.**

G. Obtaining the Prospects

It is important if we are going to effectively train our people that we provide them with the best possible source of prospects. To deal consistently with only the most difficult type of individuals is most certainly going to discourage the average beginner. We have found from our experience that the best sources of prospects are the following:

1. People who have visited our worship services. These are even better prospects than those who send their children to Sunday School without bothering themselves to attend church. Generally speaking, I would say that these are the easiest people with whom to deal. Their hearts are further prepared by a few weeks of sitting under the ministry of the Word.

   The best prospects

   Some will say, however, "We do not have many visitors come to our church." This objection was raised by a minister in one of the evangelism schools that I was conducting. I asked him how many visitors he did have. He said, "We may have two or three on any given Sunday." I then asked him how many people he had going out to present to them the Gospel. He said, "Oh, I have no one doing that," to which I responded, "Well, then, you already have two or three visitors too many." There was a time when we had only a handful of people coming to church and very few visitors, but you can begin with the visitors that you do have. We have found that the number of visitors has increased as the enthusiasm engendered by this program has increased.

How to get more visitors

In seeking to increase the number of visitors coming to church, we may ask ourselves the question: "What causes people to visit a church?" In a survey conducted at our church we asked about 1,000 people why they came to our church for the first time. The overwhelming majority said that some member of the church had invited them. This, then, is one of the big secrets of getting people to come to church—encouraging your members to invite them. Periodic Visitors Sundays with perhaps some coffee served afterward and a special emphasis for several weeks beforehand to invite their friends is a fruitful source of prospects. An enthusiastic congregation will provide more than enough people to talk to about Christ.

Sunday school

2. A second source of prospects would be the parents of children who attend Sunday school. This source, however, will not prove very fruitful unless Sunday school teachers have had an active program of visiting in the homes and showing an interest in the children's progress in their Christian education. If this has been done, however, the parents will be generally open to the Gospel.

New residents

3. A third source of prospects is the weekly or bi-weekly or monthly listing of those who have bought new homes in the area. This can be obtained from some source in almost every city. Any real estate salesman in the congregation can usually tell you where to obtain it. In Fort Lauderdale it costs $75 per year, but it is worth many times that to any church. We begin by sending a friendly letter to these people welcoming them into the community and offering our services in any way possible. We conclude the letter by stating that we hope

someone from the church will be able to drop by in the near future and welcome them personally to our area and to our church. A card is then made out for them showing the date of the letter and indicating that they are a new resident in the area. They are then processed in the visitation program.

4. A fourth source of prospects, if the first three fail to provide an adequate number, is a house-to-house religious survey and opinion poll. The most effective type, I believe, is one wherein you begin with general census-type questions and lead gradually into questions that deal with the individual's needs and interest. We have found it helpful to lead into the question, "Have you come to the place in your spiritual life where you know for sure that you have eternal life?" If the answer to that is "no," it may be followed by the question, "Would you like for me to share with you how you could know?"

House-to-house survey

These questions will sift the general population and help you to find the people who have a genuine interest in spiritual matters. As has been said many times, "There is no sense in tugging at green fruit."

Green fruit

H. Presenting the Gospel

Our basic approach is neither apologetic, defensive, or negative. It is a simple, positive statement of the **Good News of the Gospel.** We have found that most Christians do not know how to make an intelligible, forceful and interesting presentation of the Gospel. This is basically what we are trying to teach them to do.

Positive approach

We feel that a very useful tool which is often omitted from texts on evangelism is an actual presentation of the Gospel itself. Such a presentation is included in the training materials, and the people are encouraged to learn it and use it as a

Written presentation

15

guide as they begin to present the Gospel of Christ. Later it is no doubt adapted to the individual personality with many additions or subtractions, as the case may require. But most people need something with which to start.

Basic training

The essential things which we are trying to teach our people are: how to get into the Gospel and find out where the person is spiritually, how to present the Gospel itself, and how to bring the person to a commitment to Jesus Christ at the conclusion.

Three parts of Gospel

In teaching the trainees the presentation of the Gospel (II in the Outline), we proceed in the following manner. First, we have them learn the **Outline of the Gospel,** which might be considered as the **skeleton.** Secondly, we have them learn **Scripture verses** which give **muscle,** so to speak, to the outline. Thirdly, we have them learn **illustrations** which **flesh out** and make clear and understandable the Outline of the Gospel.

Build on Outline

In having the trainees learn the Gospel, we do not have them memorize the entire presentation but rather have them learn the Outline and then gradually **build on to it.** First we have them learn just enough so the "bones" of the Outline don't rattle. Then we have them give a three-minute presentation of the Gospel. And then we enlarge it to five minutes and then to eight. We continue to enlarge the presentation until they are able to present the Gospel in one minute or one hour, depending on what the particular situation warrants. We provide them with the long presentation of the Gospel, as well as the short one, which is used as resource material for building their presentation on the basic Outline. In this way it be-

Make it their own

comes their own. We encourage them to work on it, practice it, give it, until indeed they own it and can give it with authority.

I. Preserving the Fruit

A program of evangelism such as this generates a tremendous need for follow-up. It has produced a need for a follow-up secretary and also a follow-up minister on our staff, but the main responsibility for follow-up rests with the individual who has led the person to Christ. In this training workbook we have a rather elaborate section on follow-up principles and procedures. In essence the follow-up procedure involves several individual return visits wherein the new convert is established in the Scriptures and assured of his salvation. We use a variety of materials and recommend highly the Navigator follow-up materials. After several personal visits we then endeavor to get them into a small Bible Study group which will consist of several more mature Christians plus four or five newer Christians. These classes of six or eight people then provide the **spiritual incubator** in which the newborn babe will live out the first few months of his Christian life.

Follow-up procedures are not completed until the convert has been taught to study God's Word, to pray, to live the Christian life, and to walk with Christ. Then he is encouraged to come into the evangelism program to learn how to win others to Christ. Yet at this point the follow-up still is not complete, for he must be taught not only **how to reproduce** but also **how to disciple** his new convert until he has matured to the place where he also is able to bring someone else to Christ. This emphasis of **spiritual multiplication,** looking past the first generation to the second, third, and fourth is the secret of an expanding and multiplying evangelistic ministry. In just a few years this has produced instances of great, great, great, great, great, great, great grandchildren in the faith. The acid test of any follow-up procedure will ultimately be: **Is it producing spiritual grandchildren and great grandchildren? If not, then something is amiss and somewhere the process is breaking down.**

Importance of follow-up

Individual and group follow-up

Spiritual grandchildren

17

J. Multiplying the Results

A vision for the world

Christ said, "The field is the world." I believe that **our field should be the world;** that every church, every individual has a worldwide responsibility. I do not believe that any church can settle for anything less than worldwide evangelism as its own responsibility. Is it utterly unrealistic? I think not. Eleven men, indeed a very small church, have succeeded in carrying the Gospel to most every nation on the earth. And the march of those 11 men goes on today. I do not believe, however, that it necessarily must take hundreds or thousands of years for the impact of the Gospel to spread around the world. **The process of spiritual multiplication can grow with the rapidity of the physical population explosion that we are seeing today.** Our goal then is to reach the world for Christ. **How can this be done?**

Multiplying your ministry

First we must realize that **our responsibility extends beyond our church, our city, our state or the United States.** But how are we to meet this responsibility? We have proceeded in this manner. In addition to training an increasing number of people in our own church (in our last class we had 298 individuals), we have also trained a good many other churches in the city and the immediate area. Also, we have an annual clinic in February where we have been training 100 or more ministers for five days both in the classroom and in "on-the-job" training, going out with our trained laymen. This has proved very successful and hundreds of ministers have gone back to their churches with a new vision for evangelism and a new zeal for training their people to do the work of ministry.

Hold your own clinic

There are now churches all over the United States which are building programs of lay evangelism as a result of these clinics. But this does not yet meet the need. After these ministers have trained their people to become evangelists **we encourage them to have their own clinics,** inviting ministers

18

of other churches in their sphere of influence to come and learn from their people in order that they may go back and train their members, and even further, to hold their clinics and invite other ministers, so that the multiplication procedure may continue.

Our first daughter clinic was held with 40 ministers involved in a church in Michigan. Others followed, and the process continues. This program has jumped the boundaries of the United States and such programs are being conducted in a number of other nations. As this is being written, the program is being introduced in Japan. We hope that in the not too distant future there will be churches in every nation which will see the vision of training their laymen and then bringing in other ministers and teaching them to train their people until a vast army of tens of millions of Christian lay evangelists has been raised up. **This is our goal. This is our challenge.** And by the continual supply of the Spirit of Christ we trust that it shall be done.

Soli deo gloria.

The evangelism explosion!

A PRESENTATION OF THE GOSPEL

A. Outline of the Gospel Presentation

I. The Introduction
- A. Their secular life
- B. Their church background
- C. Our church
- D. Testimony: personal or church
- E. Two Questions:
  1. Have you come to a place in your spiritual life where you know for certain that if you were to die today you would go to heaven?
  2. Suppose that you were to die tonight and stand before God and He were to say to you, "Why should I let you into My heaven?" What would you say?

II. The Gospel
- A. Grace
  1. Heaven is a free gift
  2. It is not earned or deserved
- B. Man
  1. Is a sinner
  2. Cannot save himself
- C. God
  1. Is merciful—therefore doesn't want to punish us.
  2. Is just—therefore must punish sin
- D. Christ
  1. Who He is—the infinite God-man
  2. What He did—He paid for our sins and purchased a place in heaven for us which He offers as a gift which may be received by . . .
- E. Faith
  1. What it is not—mere intellectual assent nor temporal faith
  2. What it is—"trusting in Jesus Christ alone for our salvation"

III. The Commitment
- A. The qualifying question
- B. The commitment question
- C. The clarification of commitment
- D. The prayer of commitment
- E. The assurance of salvation

B. A Brief Presentation of the Gospel

I. Introduction

(Condensed, eight-minute presentation starting with the Two Questions and including part of the Commitment.)

Question 1

Well, that's very interesting, Sue, but tell me, have you come to a place in your spiritual life where you can say you know for certain that if you were to die today you would go to heaven?

I didn't think anyone could really know that!

I didn't know myself for many years but then I discovered something wonderful! I discovered it was possible to know for sure! I even discovered that this was the reason the Bible was written. The Scripture says, "These things are written that ye may know that ye have eternal life." Would you like for me to share with you how I came to the place that I knew for sure I was going to heaven?

Yes, I really would.

Question 2

Fine! I'll be happy to. First, let me ask you another question which I think really brings this whole matter into focus and which clarifies our thinking about it greatly. A minister said to me one time, "Suppose that you were to die today and stand before God and He were to say to you, 'Why should I let you into My heaven?' what would you say?" That's a good question, isn't it, Sue?

Yes, it is.

I would be interested in what you would say to that, Sue.

I can't think of any answer offhand.

I know you don't have a thesis prepared on this subject but just offhand what comes to your mind? What do you <u>think</u> you would say?

22

Well, I've tried to live a good life and I've tried to keep the Ten Commandments. I even try to live by the Golden Rule.

Well, that's fine, Sue. Those things are all very commendable. You know something, Sue, when you answered that first question I thought I had some really good news for you. And after hearing your answer to the second question I know that I do. In fact I would go so far as to say that in the next 60 seconds you are going to hear the greatest good news that you have ever heard in your whole life! That's quite a statement, isn't it?

It certainly is.

Let's see if I can back it up. All my life I felt exactly as you did. I thought if I was ever to get to heaven I'd have to earn it. I'd have to become good enough, and work for it and deserve it. And then I discovered something that absolutely amazed me. I discovered that according to the Bible **heaven is absolutely a free gift**—it is unearned, unworked for, unmerited, and undeserved. It's free! Isn't that tremendous? Let me show you a Scripture verse in the New Testament. It's Romans 6:23. Here it is. Just read it for yourself.

"The wages of sin is death, but the gift of God is eternal life through Jesus Christ our Lord."

"The gift of God is eternal life . . . " Isn't that amazing? You're probably thinking, "How can that be? Who gets it? How can we know that we have it?" Let me see if I can show you not only that this is the way it is but this is the only way it could be.

The Bible teaches that all of us have sinned, that there is none of us good enough to get into heaven because God's standard is perfection! If we were to be good enough, Jesus says we would have to

Good news

II. The Gospel
  A. Grace
    1. Heaven is a gift.
    2. Not earned or deserved.
    Romans 6:23

B. Man
  1. A sinner

be perfect. "Be ye therefore perfect, even as your Father which is in heaven is perfect. . . . But all have sinned and come short of the glory of God." In our thoughts, in our words, in our deeds—we have all failed to keep His commandments all of the time. This is the reason that none of us can earn our way into heaven. We can't save ourselves. The Bible says, "By grace are ye saved through faith . . . not of works, lest any man should boast."

2. Cannot save himself

The problem of man trying to save himself becomes even more acute when we look at what the Bible says about God. We know that God is merciful and loving, but the same Bible says that God is just and holy and righteous; that He is of purer eyes than to look upon iniquity; that He must punish sin. Of course, we know the Bible teaches that God is loving and merciful and gracious. He doesn't want to punish us. He must deal with **sin** but He doesn't want to punish **us** because He loves us. Now what is the answer to that dilemma? God in His infinite wisdom devised a solution. God sent His Son into the world to solve this problem for man.

C. God
1. Loving and merciful— does not want to punish us
2. Just—therefore must punish sin

D. Jesus Christ
1. Who He is— the infinite God-man

Now, who is Jesus Christ? According to the Bible, Jesus Christ is God, the second person of the Trinity, the Creator of the universe. The Bible says, "In the beginning was the Word and the Word was with God, and the Word was God . . . the Word became flesh and dwelt among us." God came down in human flesh.

2. What He did— paid for our sins and purchased heaven for us, which He offers as a gift

What did He come to do? The whole Bible is about one great transaction. Imagine this book in my hand contains a minutely detailed account of our life: everything we've ever done, all of our sins, all of our thoughts, all of our motives, everything we've ever done in secret—all are recorded in this book. The Bible says that some day the books will be opened and everybody will know all about us. That's going to be a red-faced day for many! I am convinced of one thing: if any man is

24

judged according to the things recorded in the book of his life he will be condemned. This (hold up the book) is our problem, you see, our sin. Here is our sin upon us like a great burden. (Place the book on the palm of one hand.) This keeps us out of heaven. This prevents us from rising up to God. What's going to be done with that? In the Old Testament God's provision for sin was described in all the foreshadowings and types. **John the Baptist announced that God's Lamb had finally come. Then Jesus Christ fulfilled the mission that was His.** What was it? Simply, it is described in one text: "All we like sheep have gone astray; we have turned every one to his own way; and the Lord hath laid on Him the iniquity of us all." Suppose my other hand here represents Jesus Christ. **The Bible says God placed all our sins on Jesus.** (Transfer the book to the "Jesus" hand.) He has laid to the account of Christ our guilt, our sin—the sin which God hates. **God has imputed or laid upon Christ our sins.** And then I read something which as a father really astounded me. I read, "It pleased the Lord to bruise Him . . . He was smitten of God and afflicted." God poured out all of His wrath for sin on His own Son. **Christ in our place, as our substitute, paid the penalty for sin.**

And He says that He goes to prepare a place for us. **He purchased a place for us in heaven.** You know, Sue, the wonderful thing is that this place in heaven Christ purchased for us He offers to us freely as a gift. "The gift of God is eternal life." By His grace He freely offers to give to us this **gift of heaven.**

How do we receive it? "By grace are ye saved through faith . . . " **Faith is the key that opens the door to heaven.** Someone said that faith is the hand of a beggar reaching out to accept the gift of a king. Let's see if we can understand that better. Many people think they have faith but they really don't know what it is. Let's see what **faith is not.** Many people believe that Jesus lived and

E. Faith
  1. **What it is not —mere intellectual assent**

nor temporal faith

died and rose again. And they suppose that this is faith. But this is merely an **intellectual assent to certain historical facts.** The Bible teaches us that even the devil believes in Christ in this way. But that won't do. Other people think that they have faith in Christ, but when you ask them what they really mean they are only trusting in Christ for the **temporal things** of life, such as health, or their children, or their finances, or strength, or guidance—the things that have to do only with this life and time that we live right here. But what the Bible means by **faith is trusting in Jesus Christ alone for our salvation—resting our hope of eternal life in Christ.** Christ didn't come down here merely to get us through an appendicitis operation or to get us safely on a plane to New York! **Christ came to get us to heaven that we might have eternal life.**

2. What it is— trusting Jesus Christ alone for salvation

Faith is trusting Jesus Christ ALONE for our salvation. People can trust in only two things. And I was trusting in the same thing that you were—in my own efforts to try to live a good enough life. Then I realized that if I could get myself to heaven in this way I would save myself; and if I could save myself I would be my saviour; and if I were my saviour then I would be in competition with Jesus Christ who claimed to be the Saviour of the world. What I needed to do was to **cease trusting in myself and start trusting in Jesus Christ.** And so seventeen years ago I did just that and I received the gift of eternal life. I didn't deserve it then and I don't deserve it now.

What, then, is the motive for living a Christian life? The motive for Christian living is **gratitude** for what Christ has given to us. The Bible says that "the love of Christ constrains us." A former president of Princeton put it this way in a book that I read. He said that as a young man he accepted Christ and the gift of eternal life. All the rest of his life was simply a P.S. to that day, saying, "Thank You, Lord, for what You gave to me then."

26

Sue, **does that make sense to you?**

Oh, yes, that's wonderful!

You've just heard the **greatest story** ever told, about the **greatest offer** ever made, by the **greatest Person** who ever lived.

Now the question is this: **Do you want to receive this gift of eternal life that Christ left heaven and died on a cross to give you?**

Oh, yes, I do.

C. An Extended Presentation of the Gospel

[An extended Presentation of the Gospel containing many extra illustrations and scriptural texts which may be used as a resource for building shorter presentations upon the basic Outline.]

(A knock at the door.)

Good morning, Mrs. Tucker. I'm Dr. Kennedy from Coral Ridge Presbyterian Church. May we come in and visit with you a while?

Why, hello. Please do come in.

Thank you. This is Mary Jones and George Simon of our church. We were so happy to have you visit our church and wanted to become better acquainted with you.

That's real nice of you.

May we sit over here? Fine. Thank you. This is a lovely home you have. That painting is most interesting. It seems to radiate peacefulness and contentment. Did you paint it yourself?

Oh, no. A friend did it for me just before we moved here. We have enjoyed it.

III. Commitment
   A. The Qualifying Question

   B. The Commitment Question

I. Introduction
   A. Secular life

27

Where did you move from, Mrs. Tucker?

Virginia.

Virginia! I thought I noticed a bit of Virginia accent.

I don't doubt it.

Do they really say "aboot the hoouse" up there?

Yes, they do.

Do they really? Let me hear you say "about the house."

Lookoout, there's a moouse in the hoouse!

That's very interesting. I've always enjoyed listening to people with Virginia accents. Tell me a little more about yourself. How did you happen to move down here?

We vacationed in this area several times and just loved it. When my husband retired we came down and looked around one summer and settled in Fort Lauderdale. We just love it here.

Do you really? It is a beautiful city, isn't it?

Yes, it is.

B. Their church background

What church did you attend back in Virginia?

Presbyterian.

The Presbyterian church? Well, I knew there was something nice about you.

Thank you. I was a charter member.

Were you really? You had the joys of seeing a new congregation born and you helped it grow.

Yes, some of those days were pretty trying but we got our problems ironed out and it is a large church now. I was president of the Women of the Church for two years and taught a Sunday School class for a while.

Fine. It's good to meet someone who is really active in the life of the church. We are truly delighted to have you here in Fort Lauderdale with us now. **How did you happen to attend our church?**

C. Our church

We were looking for a church in the neighborhood and while driving around we saw your building.

Is that a fact? How did you like the service?

Oh, we liked it very well. The first time we visited the people seemed so friendly and made us feel at home. The singing is just wonderful. You people seem to really enjoy singing. Somehow the spirit was different.

Is that right? You noticed something different about the congregation?

Yes, we did.

Do you have any idea what causes that difference?

No, but I'd like to know.

Let me share with you what I think it is. You know, many people have mentioned to me that they sense something different about our church. They noticed the singing, as you did. They saw something different about the expression on people's faces—as if they were happier. Is this the sort of difference you were thinking of?

D. Testimony
   1. Church
      (as here)
        or
   2. Personal

Yes.

The secret of that difference is really rather simple when you look at it closely. We live in very chaotic and uncertain times, don't we?

29

We certainly do.

Many people are disturbed about war and the possibility of nuclear war. People are seeking. They are searching for something to put their anchor into. A lot of these people go to church seeking something of this sort. The pathetic thing is that many times they don't find it there. At our church we have decided that, as God gives us the grace and wisdom, we are going to stick to those basic essential facts that the Christian Church is here to proclaim: the historic Christian faith. As you know, **the reason Christ put His Church in the world is that men and women might have eternal life.** Isn't that right?

Yes.

This is the reason the Church exists. Of course, it does many other things, but this is the main **reason** for its existence. In fact, where else are you going to turn for eternal life? You can't get it from some government agency——even the Great Society can't provide eternal life. It is only through the Church of Jesus Christ that we have any hope of finding eternal life. And yet we have found by talking to hundreds and hundreds of people that most people don't know whether they have eternal life. I have found that the vast majority of people don't know for certain what would happen to them if they were to die. They have hopes but they don't know for sure that they would go to heaven if they died. For many years I was the same way. I didn't know. I was striving but I really didn't know for sure. May I ask you a question, Mrs. Tucker?

Yes.

E. Two Questions
1. "Have you come to a place in your spiritual life where you know for cer-

Have you come to a place in your spiritual life where you know for certain that if you were to die today you would go to heaven?

Why, I don't think anyone can really know.

30

You don't think anyone can really know. You know, that's just the way I felt about it. For many years I didn't know. I wasn't even aware of the fact that anybody knew. But let me tell you some really good news: **It is possible to know** and there are a great many people who do know.

Really?

That was an amazing discovery to me! In fact I even learned that that was the reason the Bible was written! The Bible says: "These things have I written . . . that ye may know that ye have eternal life."

Why, I never knew that!

I didn't either. Isn't that a fantastic thing! Think how wonderful it would be if you could go to bed tonight and lay your head on your pillow knowing for certain that if you don't wake up in your bedroom, you will wake up in heaven with Christ. Wouldn't that be a wonderful thing to know?

Yes, it really would.

Would you like me to share with you how I came to know that I have eternal life and will go to heaven and be with Christ when I die?

Yes, please do.

All right. I'll be happy to, for it is the greatest discovery that I have ever made. It really has changed my whole life. I wouldn't trade everything else in the world for this wonderful discovery and the joy of sharing it with other people. You know, it's amazing how many people are hungry for these things! I talk to people in all strata of society and everywhere there are men and women eager to know, and yet no one has ever taken the time to explain these things to them.

tain that if you were to die today you would go to heaven?"

31

I've never heard it.

2. "Suppose that you were to die tonight and stand before God and He were to say to you, 'Why should I let you into My heaven?' What would you say?"

Before I get into it, let me ask you another question. I think this really crystallizes our thinking on the matter. This was a question that was very helpful to me. A minister asked me this one day: **"Suppose that you were to die today and stand before God and He were to say to you, 'Why should I let you into My heaven?' What do you think you would say?"** That's a pretty good question, isn't it?

It certainly is.

It really makes you think. What do you think you would say? What would your answer be?

Well, I never thought of anything like that. I've gone to Sunday School and church all my life. And I try to be as good as I know how. Of course, I know that I haven't always been perfect, but I don't think I've ever intentionally hurt anyone. And I try to love my neighbor. I don't think I've been too bad.

All right. Anything else?

Well, I visit the sick and I do the very best I can to live according to the Golden Rule.

Well, thank you, Mrs. Tucker. It's Rene, isn't it? May I call you that?

Yes.

Good news

You know, Rene, when I asked you if you knew for sure if you had eternal life and you said that you didn't, I thought I had some really good news to tell you. And after your answer to that second question, **I know that I do!** In fact, I would say that in the next few minutes **you are going to hear the greatest good news that you've ever heard in all your life.** That's quite a statement to make, isn't it?

32

It certainly is.

Well, let me see if I can back it up. You know, all my life I felt exactly like you did. I thought that heaven was something I had to earn; in some way I had to merit it or pay for it; of course, not with the paper currency that we use here, but with the currency of heaven which I figured was good works, morality, piety, character, and that sort of thing. I supposed that if I piled up these things that somehow, someday, I might earn my right to go in. Then I discovered something that absolutely amazed me. I discovered that heaven is not something that you earn, or that you deserve, or that you work for, but that, **according to the Scriptures, heaven—eternal life—is absolutely a free gift!**

Free?

Absolutely free! Isn't that amazing?

Oh, yes!

It's unearned, unworked for, unstriven for, undeserved, and unmerited. It's free. You know, we sort of think there's nothing in this life that's free. We always look for the price tag. And that's probably true. But thanks be unto God that the greatest thing that man could ever need—eternal life—is free! Of course the idea that we have to pay for everything is something which is ingrained in us from our earliest days. This is the way which seems right to every man. In fact, most people think they're going to get to heaven that way. It's the way that seems right to every man, isn't it?

Yes, it is.

The Bible says this: "There is a way which seemeth right unto a man (and that's this) but (it also says) the end thereof are the ways of death." God says that His ways are not our ways and as high as the heavens are above the earth, so high

II. The Gospel

A. Grace

1. Heaven is a free gift

Rom 6:23 "the gift of God is eternal life through Jesus Christ our Lord."

2. It is not earned or deserved

Titus 3:5 "Not by works of righteousness which we have done."

Man's ways are not God's ways

Romans 6:23

33

are His ways above our ways and His thoughts above our thoughts. **God's way is the way of grace.** He is the God of all grace. Rene, let me show you a Scripture verse in the New Testament. This is found in **Romans 6:23.** You see what it says? "For the wages (wages, of course, are what we earn, what we deserve) of sin (and we're all sinners) is death (physical death, spiritual death, eternal death) BUT (and here's the good news) the gift of God is eternal life through Jesus Christ our Lord." "The gift of God is eternal life." Isn't that amazing, Rene?

That's wonderful!

Why, it's the most wonderful thing that I've ever heard in all of my life! Well, I'm sure that this raises many questions in your mind. "How can these things be? How can God do this and still be just? And who gets the gift, after all? Everybody?" Well, not at all. In fact, **Christ said that few there are that find the way and many there are which go in to destruction.** Well, if everybody doesn't get the gift, who does get it? How do we get it? And how can we know if we have it? Now, Rene, let me see if I can answer these questions for you. In fact, I think I can show you not only that this is the way, but when you understand what the Bible teaches concerning man and concerning God, I think you will see that this is not only the way it is, but that this is the way it must be.

B. Man
  1. A sinner
"For all have sinned and come short of the glory of God."
  Romans 3:23
"As it is written, there is none righteous, no, not one."
  Romans 3:10

The first thing I came to understand was what God says about man in the Bible. This is a practical place to begin because it brings us face to face with the predicament in which man finds himself—and a real predicament it is! **According to God's Word, man has made a colossal mess out of everything he has put his hands on.** If we were to get away from this planet and look at it objectively, we would appreciate the truth of this teaching. We have wars and riots; we have crime and delinquency; we have murder and hatred and

34

envy and strife. According to the Bible, **all of these are the result of sin.** This is the fatal malignancy which infects the soul of the entire human race. The Bible says, "There is none righteous, no, not one . . . for all have sinned and come short of the glory of God. There is not a just man upon the face of the earth that doeth good and sinneth not. We have turned every one to his own way." The Bible teaches that all of us have sinned, right?

I know that.

This is a very black picture. In fact, the Bible paints it even darker. It is against this backdrop that we must see the glorious picture of the Gospel. Sin is a cancer destroying the human race and cannot be dealt with effectively until it is openly acknowledged. In thought, word, and deed we have all come short of the standard God has set for us. **Jesus said that sin in thought is the same as sin in deed.** "Ye have heard it said . . . whosoever shall kill shall be in danger of the judgment . . . but I say that whosoever is angry with his brother without a cause shall be in danger of the judgment. Ye have heard that it was said . . . thou shalt not commit adultery; but I say . . . whosoever looketh on a woman to lust after her hath committed adultery. . . . " The Bible says, "Ye have heard that it hath been said, thou shalt love thy neighbor . . . but I say unto you, love your enemies, bless them that curse you, do good to them that hate you, and pray for them that despitefully use you . . . that ye may be the children of your Father which is in heaven." Jesus made it very plain. He said, "Did not Moses give you the Commandments and none of you has kept them?"

The Bible teaches that we have not kept God's Commandments but have broken them all; if not in deed, at least in thought and word. We have not lived by the Golden Rule all the time. We have not really done the best we can. **There are not**

"There is none that understandeth, there is none that seeketh after God."

Romans 3:11

"They are all gone out of the way, they are together become unprofitable, there is none that doeth good, no, not one."

Romans 3:12

Word, thought or deed

Omission or commission

35

only sins of commission, in word, thought and deed, but according to the Bible, there are also sins of omission: those things which we should have done that we have not—failing to pray or read the Bible, or to truly love our neighbor, or to go to church. The Bible says these are all sins.

Sometimes I wonder just how many times a day I sin. I imagine it's 50 to 100 times or even more. John Calvin said no one knows the one-hundredth part of the sin that clings to his soul. Today a psychologist would tell us that we have forgotten 99 percent of all those things we have ever done wrong. We suppress them because we don't like to think about the unpleasant. Just suppose that we sinned only 10 times a day or even 5—or even just 3. Why, we would practically be walking angels! Imagine if no oftener than three times a day did we think unkind thoughts, or lose our temper, or fail to do what we ought towards God and man—we would be pretty fine people, would we not? Even if we were this good, we would still have over 1,000 transgressions a year! Multiply that by our own age and we find twenty- thirty- forty- fifty-thousand violations of the Law of God on our records. Think what would happen to an habitual offender in a criminal court with 30,000 transgressions on his record!

2. Cannot save himself
"Not by works of righteousness which we have done but according to His mercy He saved us."
Titus 3:5
"Not of works, lest any man should boast."
Ephesians 2:9

This impresses us with man's predicament. According to the Bible he is a sinner. He has broken God's Law. The Bible goes on to teach that our predicament is compounded by another factor that is understood by fewer people. Because man is a sinner, he cannot earn his way into heaven. That is, he cannot merit eternal life by doing good things. The Bible states this clearly. "Not by works of righteousness which we have done but according to His mercy He saved us." "By grace are ye saved through faith . . . not of works lest any man should boast."

There was a time when I thought I could get to heaven by keeping the Ten Commandments, living according to the Golden Rule, and helping people less fortunate than myself. However, occasionally I would wonder just how well I would have to do all these things to get into heaven. It was sort of like wondering in school, what is the passing grade in my classes? Well, **God has told us how well we have to do these works to get into heaven.** He has revealed the passing grade in his class of life. **Do you know what it is?**

No.

All right. Hold on to your chair! Are you ready? Here it comes! Jesus said: "Be ye therefore perfect, even as your Father in heaven is perfect."

Perfect?

There it stands! That's the passing grade! The amazing thing I discovered is that God doesn't grade on a curve. God says, "Be ye . . . PERFECT." This is not an isolated text that might be interpreted in some other way, but this is something that is taught throughout the Bible. For example, Paul said, "Cursed is every one that continueth not in all things which are written in the book of the law to do them." If we don't continually do everything that we are told to do, then we are under the curse of God. James put it another way: "If we offend in one point we are guilty of all." If we commit just one sin we step outside the realm of the law and become an outlaw. You don't have to break every law in the book to be an outlaw and have the police looking for you; just one crime is all it takes to have a lot of policemen looking for us. One sin is all that it takes to make us guilty and to make us an outlaw. Just one sin! Satan thought just one evil thought and because of that he was cast out of heaven.

Well, then, no one's going to be able to go to heaven!

"There is a way which seemeth right unto a man, but the end thereof are the ways of death."
Proverbs 14:12

It would look that way, wouldn't it? You see, what we have said is that your understanding (which is the same as mine used to be) is simply that a person gets to heaven by trying to be good enough. Now, boiling it all down, that is what you've come to understand all your life, right?

Yes.

None good enough

Just like I did. But the problem is: **What is good enough?** The Bible makes it plain that **good enough is perfect!** There is no doubt about that fact. Yet we have all sinned, because the same Bible also says that " . . . there is none righteous, no, not one . . . for all have sinned and come short of the glory of God." This presents a problem, doesn't it? It does look as though nobody is going to heaven.

That's right.

Impossibility of salvation by works

Well, that is right——if this is the way that you get to heaven! **Martin Luther said that the most damnable and pernicious heresy that has ever plagued the mind of man was the idea that somehow he could make himself good enough to deserve to live with an all-holy God.** We couldn't make an omelet out of three good eggs and three rotten eggs and serve it to company and expect it to be acceptable! Well, even less can we serve up our lives to God, which may have many things in them that men would call good, and yet are filled with deeds and thoughts that are rotten, and expect them to be acceptable to God. If we want to get to heaven by our good works, then all we have to do is be perfect. God's standard is complete obedience to Him at all times——and all of us have fallen short of this. We just don't have the wherewithal to pay for eternal life. Queen Elizabeth of England offered her doctor half the British empire for six months of life when she was dying. Of course, her doctor couldn't give her six seconds. How much less, then, can we buy eternal life from God by our good works.

38

If anybody is going to be in heaven then there must be some entirely different way of getting there. The Bible, of course, says that there are going to be people in heaven. Might I add that Jesus made it plain that the number of people in heaven will be a minority of those that have lived upon the earth. "Straight is the gate, and narrow is the way, which leadeth unto life, and FEW there be that find it . . . for wide is the gate, and broad is the way that leadeth to destruction, and MANY there be which go in thereat." This "few" is a great multitude that no man can number, but seemingly it is the lesser part of mankind, which makes us realize that we can't just take it for granted. Trusting in our own efforts to be good obviously will not get us to heaven. This was the religion of the Pharisees. Do you remember? Jesus described them in this way: "They trusted in themselves that they were righteous." Many people have this belief today. In talking of these matters with literally hundreds of people, I found the vast majority indicate they intend to enter heaven on the basis of their own good works. The Bible teaches, "There is a way that seemeth right unto man." It would appear that this is the way that seems right unto man. But the Bible continues, "the end thereof are the ways of death." So then there must be another way. What is it? Well, to understand it we have to move on from our consideration of what God has said about us to what He says about Himself. About us, He has said we are sinners and we can do nothing to remedy our sinful condition.

One of the most amazing and most difficult facts to learn is that God loves us in spite of what we are. He loves us not because of what we are but because of what He is. For the Bible tells us that "God is love." This love of God becomes all the more incomprehensible when we have come to see ourselves as we truly are. Then we feel like crying out with the great hymnist, Charles Wesley:

"And can it be that I should gain/An in-

An entirely different way

C. God
   1. Loving and
      merciful
"He that loveth not, knoweth not God; for God is love."
I John 4:8

39

"Yea, I have loved
thee with an everlast-
ing love."
      Jeremiah 31:3
   2. Just—there-
      fore must pun-
      ish sin
"Then will I visit their
transgression with the
rod and their iniquity
with stripes."
      Psalm 89:32
"God will by no means
clear the guilty."
      Exodus 34:7b

terest in the Saviour's blood? Died He for me, who caused His pain? For me, who Him to death pursued? Amazing love! how can it be/ That Thou, my God, shouldst die for me?"

How vast! How measureless is this love of God to us!

About Himself, God says, "I am holy and just and righteous. I am of purer eyes than to behold iniquity. The soul that sinneth it shall die." We are looking at man's problems through the magnifying glass of God—as it is seen by an all-holy, sin-hating God who says He is angry with the wicked all the day. Because He is a just Judge, He must punish our sins. His law declares that our sins must be punished: "He will by no means clear the guilty." He threatens to visit our transgressions with the rod. There is no doubt about this—**God will certainly punish ALL sin.**

In our hearts we would view with contempt a judge who is overly lenient with offenders. If one were to "slap the wrist" of his friend who was guilty of a heinous crime, we would cry, "Impeach him. Justice must be preserved." So it is with God. "Shall not the Judge of all the earth do right?"

   I thought God was mostly love.

He is both holy and loving. It is interesting to note that for many centuries before He revealed the real height of His love in Jesus Christ, He established that His throne is a throne of righteousness. He is the thrice-holy One who will deal with sin. Throughout the Old Testament His justice and holiness is clearly manifested.

If He were only justice we would all be condemned. However, He is loving and merciful. **Although He must punish sin, He loves us and therefore doesn't want to punish us.** If He were only loving, there would be no problem. If He were the grandfather figure, as most Americans picture Him, He could just take us all to heaven —all of us: Dillinger and Capone, Nero and Judas, and the devil himself. He would simply say, "Come on, fellows, I didn't really mean it when I said, 'The soul that sinneth, it shall die.'" No! **Any loving dealings that God has with us must be consonant with His justice.**

The teachings that God emphasizes about Himself are: **He is holy and just and must punish sin; but He is also loving and merciful and does not want to punish us.** In effect, this created a problem for God which He solved in Jesus Christ.

Now, what is the answer to that problem? God in His infinite wisdom devised a solution. **Jesus Christ is God's answer to the predicament.** He sent His Son into the world and, as you know, we celebrate His birth every Christmas. Rene, I would be interested in your opinion about Christ. Who do you think He is?

> Well, He was probably the best man that ever lived. He was a wonderful teacher and I believe He is supposed to have worked miracles.

Fine! Jesus was a great teacher and miracle-worker. And He was good. Anything else?

> Well, He was the Son of God.

Yes, He was. What do you think that means? What do we mean when we say, "Jesus is the Son of God?"

> I don't really know.

The Bible teaches that Jesus Christ—Jesus of Nazareth, the Carpenter of Galilee—is God! He is the Creator of the world! He is the One who created the whole universe! Jesus is God Almighty, Himself! This comes as a real surprise to many

D. Jesus Christ
   **1. Who He is—
      the infinite
      God-man**

"In the beginning was the Word, and the Word was with God, and the Word was God."

       John 1:1

"For unto us a child is born, unto us a son is given: and the government shall be upon his shoulder: and his name shall be called Wonderful, Counselor, The mighty God, The everlasting Father, The Prince of Peace."

       Isaiah 9:6

"And Thomas answered and said unto him, My Lord and my God."

       John 20:28

people. They don't realize that He is God the Son—that God is Father, Son and Holy Spirit, and that the Trinity is One God. Yet we sing this truth every Sunday morning in the Doxology: "Praise God from whom all blessings flow . . . praise Father, Son and Holy Ghost." Or, as our Confession puts it, "In the unity of the Godhead, there be three Persons of one substance, power and eternity."

2. **What He did— paid for our sins and purchased heaven for us, which He offers as a gift.**

"All we like sheep have gone astray; we have turned every one to his own way; and the Lord hath laid on him the iniquity of us all."

Isaiah 53:6

"Surely he hath borne our griefs, and carried our sorrows: yet we did esteem him stricken: smitten of God, and afflicted."

Isaiah 53:4

"For the wages of sin is death; but the gift of God is eternal life through Jesus Christ our Lord."

Romans 6:23

The multitude of our sins

God the Son became man! This is what we mean by **incarnation.** This is what we celebrate at Christmas. He became man for a particular purpose. He left His home in glory and was born in the filth of a stable. He lived a perfect life. He taught the world's greatest doctrines. He worked its mightiest deeds. **Finally He came to the end of His life—to that hour for which He had come.** In that hour we see the **great transaction about which the whole Bible is written**—the great transaction which is the central fact of the Christian religion. What was it?

Let's imagine this book in my hand is a minutely detailed account of our life. It includes everything we have ever done. Every word we ever spoke; every thought that ever crossed our mind. Some day, the Bible says, the books are going to be opened and everything about our lives will be brought to light. "The hidden things of darkness will be made manifest. That which has been whispered in the ear will be shouted from the housetop." Everyone will know all about us—all we've thought or done; all our hidden motives; all the sins—most of which we have forgotten. Now how many thoughts can you remember from 1950?

None!

Psychologists tell us 10,000 thoughts go through the human mind in one day. That's 3,500,000 a year! To remember only 1 percent from 1950 you would have to come up with 35,000. If we must give an account of every idle word, how many

42

would that be? We speak millions every year. Who knows? God does! They are all written down in His book. And one day the books will be opened. I am utterly convinced of one thing: that **if any man is judged according to the things recorded in the book of his life, he will be condemned.** This (hold up a book) is our problem, you see, our sin. Here is our sin upon us like a great burden. (Place the book on the palm of one hand.) This keeps us out of heaven. This prevents us from rising up to God. What's going to be done with that?

In the Old Testament God's provision for sin was described in all the foreshadowings and types. John the Baptist announced that God's Lamb had finally come. Then, **Jesus Christ fulfilled the mission that was His.** What was it? Simply, it is described in one text: "All we like sheep have gone astray; we have turned every one to his own way; and the LORD hath laid on Him the iniquity of us all." Suppose my other hand here represents Jesus Christ. The Bible says God placed all our sins on Jesus. (Transfer the book to the "Jesus" hand.) **He has laid to the account of Christ our guilt, our sin—the sin which God hates.**

The great transaction

This sin, which must be punished, is now laid upon God's own beloved Son. "Christ bare our sin in His own body on the tree." The most astounding fact in all the world is that Christ was "smitten of God and afflicted. It pleased the Lord to bruise Him; He hath put Him to grief." This means it was the will of God the Father to punish His own beloved Son in our place, as our substitute. **The infinite Son of God became man.** A man must be punished for sin—not a goat or a bull or an angel—but a man. On the other hand, the sin of the world is an **infinite sin.** The penalty paid must be an **infinite penalty.** The sacrifice for the sins of the world must be a man who can endure an infinite penalty. **An infinite man is needed and this is Jesus Christ, the Son of God,** who became the Son of Man. He voluntarily came

The infinite God-Man

43

into the world, saying, "Father, I will take their place. I will pay their penalty. I will endure their punishment."

Christ suffered in such a way as we could never comprehend. One hymn writer said,

> "We may not know, we cannot tell/What pains He had to bear;
> But we believe it was for us/He hung and suffered there."

On the cross Jesus endured the wrath of God, the infinite wrath of God. Even the sun hid its face as the God-Man descended into hell for us. Finally, **when the last sin had been paid for, Jesus said,** "It is finished!" This is an interesting word in the original text. It is "Tetelestai," a commercial word which means "It is paid; the debt is paid." "The wages of sin is death," or the wrath of God. Jesus said, "Tetelestai. It is paid!" Further, He said, "In My Father's house are many mansions. If it were not so I would have told you. I go to prepare a place for you." It is paid. It is purchased. With His own passion on the cross, Jesus secured a place in heaven for His own people.

All my life I thought as you. If ever I was to go and dwell in heaven, I would have to deserve it. My life would have to be good enough. In other words, I would have to pay an admission price of good works to enter the door of heaven. I was amazed to learn that it's not so! **I don't have to pay for it. Jesus already paid for it and I can have eternal life as a gift.** Listen: "The wages of sin is death but the GIFT OF GOD is eternal life through Jesus Christ our Lord." **That is the Gospel, the good news of the Christian faith: God offers heaven to us as a gift. Heaven is free to us because it was paid for by Christ.**

The Bible says, "By GRACE are ye saved . . . not of works lest any man should boast." What is the

It is finished

The gift of God

44

meaning of grace? Once someone gave an acrostic: G—R—A—C—E: **G**od's **R**iches **A**t **C**hrist's **E**xpense. **God's riches:** forgiveness, heaven, eternal life, peace, joy, and a sense of the love of God—**at Christ's expense.** The expense of the scourge, Gethsemane, the mocking, the plucking of His beard, the crown of thorns, the nailing of His hands, the piercing of His side, the wrath of God, and hell itself. "Jesus paid it all. All to Him I owe." He offers us eternal life as a gift by grace.

Who receives this gift? Everybody? No. The Bible says that few find the way to life and that many go to destruction. **How can we have this gift?** This brings us to the fourth and last thing we need to understand: **We receive the gift of God by faith.** The Bible says, "By grace are ye saved THROUGH FAITH." **Faith is the key that opens the door to heaven.** You know, you could have a key ring with a lot of keys on it, like this; they all look somewhat alike. But I'll tell you this. If you go to the front door of our church, you could try all of these keys except the right one, and they would not open that door. The right key to heaven is called **faith, saving faith.** That is what will open the door to heaven. There is nothing else in the world that will open that door.

Let me tell you what the key is not. Many people mistake two things for saving faith. If you were to look at these keys you would find that there are several of them that look very similar. In fact, you might not be able at first glance to tell which was which. So it is with faith. Now, **the first thing that people mistake for saving faith is this: an intellectual assent to certain historical facts.** You believe in God, don't you?

> Yes, I always have.

You always have believed in God. So have I. But that type of belief is not what the Bible means by saving faith. I believed in God all my life but for about 25 years I was not truly saved. **The**

E. Faith

   1. What it is not
      —mere intellectual assent

"Thou believest that there is one God; thou doest well: the devils also believe and tremble."

James 2:19

(The demons speaking) "And, behold, they cried out, saying, What have we to do with Thee, Jesus, Thou Son of God? Art Thou come hither to torment us before the time?"

Matthew 8:29

Bible says the devil believes in God. Did you know that? The Bible says, "Thou believest that there is one God; thou doest well, the devils also believe and tremble." **So believing in God is not what the Bible means by saving faith.** The demons in the Gadarene demoniac said, "What have we to do with Thee, Jesus, Thou Son of God? Art Thou come hither to torment us before the time?" Even demons believe in the deity of Christ! But they evidently weren't saved! That's one thing people mistake for saving faith: an intellectual assent to the historicity of Christ, but that's not what the Bible means by faith.

. . . nor temporal faith

Let me give you one other thing that people mistake for saving faith. You have prayed to God many times, haven't you?

Oh, every day.

You've had problems that you've committed to the Lord, right? You've trusted Him for some things.

Oh, yes. I couldn't have gotten through life without prayer.

Rene, for example, what did you trust Him for?

Well, when my children were sick, when our finances were low and our business was bad —why, I've always prayed to the Lord for those things.

You see, you had more than intellectual assent. You have actually trusted Him for some things, right?

Yes.

Your children were sick. Your financial situation and your business were bad. I could probably add other things. You probably trusted Him for decisions which you had to make; you probably even prayed that He would keep you safe while

46

you traveled on a long trip. Perhaps you had an operation. You prayed to Him to bring you through that safely. Things like this.

Yes.

Now, all these are good and you should trust in the Lord for all these things. But, you see, **even this is not saving faith.** We might say that when you trusted in the Lord for your finances you had a financial-faith. You trusted in the Lord to take care of your family—you could call that family-faith. You trusted in the Lord to help you with your decisions—you might call that deciding-faith. On trips, you had traveling-faith. **There is one element all these things have in common. They are temporal,** aren't they? They are all the things of this life, things of this world that shall pass away. Now many people, I find, trust the Lord for all these temporal matters. **But saving faith is trusting Christ to save you—to save you eternally.**

I never thought of it that way.

Why, neither had I. You see, I trusted the Lord for this, and this, and for the other, but to get right down to what I was trusting in for eternal salvation—I was trusting in myself. I tried to live a good life. I tried to keep the Ten Commandments. I tried to live by the Golden Rule. I, I, I, I—you see? It was "I!" What did I ask you? —"What are you trusting in for eternal life? What are you trusting in to get into heaven?" Do you remember what you said? "I try to do the best I can. I try to live a good life according to the Golden Rule. I try to do all these things." Do you see?

Saving faith is trusting Jesus Christ ALONE for our salvation. It means resting upon Christ alone and what He has done rather than upon what I have done to get me into heaven. This is illustrated very clearly in the life of John Wesley who started the Methodist Church.

2. What it is—
Trusting in Jesus Christ alone for salvation.
"And they said, believe on the Lord Jesus Christ, and thou shalt be saved, and thy house."
Acts 16:31

"He that believeth on the Son hath everlasting life and he that believeth not the Son shall not see life; but the wrath of God abideth on him."
John 3:36

"For by grace are ye saved through faith; and that not of yourselves: it is the gift of God: Not of works, lest any man should boast."
Ephesians 2:8,9

47

He went to Oxford Seminary for five years in England and then became a minister of the Church of England where he served for about ten years. Toward the end of this time he became a missionary from England to Georgia, in approximately 1735. All of his life he had been quite a failure in his ministry though he was, as we would count men, very pious. He got up at 4 o'clock in the morning and prayed for two hours. He would then read the Bible for an hour before going to the jails, prisons, and hospitals to minister to all manner of people. He would teach, and pray for, and help others until late at night. He did this for years. In fact, the Methodist Church gets its name from the methodical life of piety that Wesley and his friends lived.

Wesley's experience

On the way back from America there was a great storm at sea. The little ship upon which they were sailing was about to sink. Huge waves broke over the ship and the wind roared in the sails. Wesley feared he was going to die that night and he was terrified. He had no assurance of what would happen to him when he died. Despite all of his efforts to be good, death now for him was just a big black question mark. On one side of the ship was a group of men who were singing hymns. He asked them, "How can you sing when this very night you are going to die?" They replied, "If this ship goes down we will go up to be with the Lord forever." Wesley went away shaking his head, thinking to himself, "How can they know that? What have they done that I have not done?" Then he added, "I came to convert the heathen, but who shall convert me?"

In the providence of God, the ship made it back to England. Wesley went to London and found his way to Aldersgate Street and a small chapel. There he heard a man reading a sermon which had been written two centuries before by Martin Luther, entitled "Luther's Preface to the Book of Romans." This sermon described what **real faith** was. It is **trusting Jesus Christ only for salvation —and not in our own good works.** Wesley suddenly realized that he had been on the wrong road all his life. That night he wrote these words in his journal: "About a quarter before nine, while he was describing the change which God works in the heart through faith in Christ, I felt my heart strangely warmed. I felt I did trust in Christ, Christ alone, for salvation; and an assurance was given me that He had taken away my sins, even mine, and saved me from the law of sin and death." There it is. That is saving faith. Trusting in Jesus Christ alone for salvation. Now, would you say that Wesley had not believed in Jesus Christ before this night? Of course, he had. He believed in Christ in English, and Latin, and Greek and Hebrew—he was a biblical scholar. But he trusted in John Wesley for his salvation. After this he became the greatest preacher of the eighteenth century. But it all began when he put his trust in Jesus Christ alone for salvation.

Let me illustrate. You see this chair over here? A lovely chair isn't it?

Resting on Christ

   Yes.

You believe that chair exists?

   Yes.

Do you believe that it would hold you up?

   Yes.

But, you see, it's not holding you up for a very simple reason: you're not sitting on it. That is the way I was with Christ. I believed Jesus existed. I believed He was divine. I trusted Him for finances and for health, as you have done too. But, you see, saving faith is trusting myself into His hands eternally. Some people will trust the Lord for their protection when they go out at night. They wouldn't think of putting out the

49

garbage at night without trusting the Lord to take care of them. But as far as their eternal welfare is concerned, they are trusting in their own efforts because they have never understood what the Bible teaches.

Saving faith is putting my trust in Jesus Christ for eternal life. Over 17 years ago I transferred my trust from myself to Jesus Christ; from what I had been doing for God to what He has done for me on the cross. By a simple act of faith I transferred my trust from what I had done to what Christ had done for me. Just as I am now transferring my trust from this chair that I have been resting on (representing my good works) to this one representing Christ. Now I'm resting on only one thing: that is, Jesus Christ. No longer am I trusting what I have done; rather, I trust what He has done for me. We've sung this in many hymns, such as, "On Christ the solid rock I stand,/ All other ground is sinking sand" . . . "Nothing in my hands I bring **(good works, prayers, church-going, loving my neighbor—nothing in my hands),**/Simply to the cross I cling." Did you ever sing this? "Just as I am without one plea, **(Just as I am—a sinner, unworthy, undeserving, without one plea)**/Except Thy blood was shed for me,/And that Thou bidst me come to Thee,/O Lamb of God, I come, I come." How amazing is the love of Christ that He is willing to receive us just as we are and to cleanse us, forgive us, and give us eternal life.

Right actions, wrong motives

Let's say that this pen in my right hand represents eternal life. There are only two relationships you can have to it. Either you have it, as this hand does, or you haven't, as this hand doesn't. Now if you don't have it and you believe it exists, you are going to want to get it. So you do the best you can; you love your neighbor, go to church, read the Bible, pray, give money, and then you say, "Lord, here are all the things I've done. I hope I've done enough to get into heaven." But

50

you see, in this case it becomes evident that everything that you've done has been for the motive of _getting_ eternal life. There is this _selfish motive_ underlying everything and so we couldn't possibly get there. Furthermore, the problem is something like that old song: "Sixteen tons and what do you get;/Another day older and deeper in debt." **We could never earn eternal life.** The Bible says that God came to earth and on the cross in the person of His Son He paid for eternal life— an infinite price. By His graciousness He offers it to us freely as a gift. It is received by faith: "Faith is the hand of a beggar reaching out to accept the gift of a King." This beggar reached out an unclean hand over 17 years ago and received the gift of eternal life. I didn't deserve it then and I don't deserve it now—nor will I ever deserve it. That's the meaning of grace.

Why, then, should I try to live a good life? The reason for living a godly life is gratitude. That's the motive for Christian living. I'm not trying to gain something I don't have by my efforts to be good; rather, I'm saying, "Thank You" for the eternal life the Lord has given me. A former president of Princeton put it this way in a book. He said that as a young man he accepted Christ and the gift of eternal life. All the rest of his life was simply a P.S. to that day, saying, "Thank You, Lord, for what You gave to me then." The motive for all is gratitude for the gift of eternal life. "The love of Christ constrains us."

Rene, **does that make sense to you?**

Oh, yes, that's beautiful!

Rene, you have just heard the greatest story ever told—the Good News, the Gospel of Jesus Christ about the greatest offer ever made. Now, Rene, the question God is asking you is simply this: **Do you want to receive the gift of eternal life?** This gift that the Son of God left His throne and went

The right motive
for Christian living

III. The Commitment

   A. The qualifying
       Question

   B. The commitment
       Question

51

to hell on the cross to procure for you, would you like to receive it?

Oh, yes, I would.

C. **The clarification of commitment**

Transfer your trust?

Would you like to transfer your trust, that is, your hope of getting into heaven, from your church attendance, your living according to the Golden Rule, **from yourself and what you have been doing, to what Christ has done for you?** Though we have completely failed to live by the Golden Rule or to keep God's Commandments, what we have failed to do, Christ has done. He has lived the perfect life. **That perfect life of Christ is imputed to us the moment we believe.** It is reckoned to our account—placed to our account—so that in the sight of God we are then accounted as perfect. Only in this way can we ever acquire that perfect standing that God requires of us. Do you want to **stop trusting Rene and start trusting Christ?**

Receive the righteousness of Christ?

Yes, I do.

Receive the resurrected and living Christ?

You receive eternal life by receiving the person of Jesus Christ. "He came unto His own and His own received Him not. But as many as received Him, to them gave He the power to become the sons of God." We can receive and know the most exciting person in the history of the world because **He is alive!** We do not worship a dead Christ but a living, glorious Saviour. The most important fact in the history of mankind is that **Jesus Christ rose from the dead.** Not only is this the most important fact, beside which all others pale into insignificance, but also it is the **best attested fact of human history.** For almost six weeks, Christ showed Himself alive to hundreds of people after His passion by many infallible proofs. For centuries men have tried to disprove the resurrection of Christ. But every effort of the skeptic has been discredited by another skeptic until the entire endeavor lies in a heap before the incontestable fact of the empty tomb. **Christ is**

alive—and He says, "Behold, I stand at the door, and knock: (the door of your life) if any one hear My voice, and open the door, I will come in to him, and will sup with him, and he with Me." This means that He will have intimate communion daily in your life. He will come in to forgive you and to cleanse you and to give you eternal life. He will come into your life and make you **His child** and an **heir** of an eternal fortune **if you receive Him.** Rene, **would you like to ask Jesus Christ to come into your life as your Saviour today?**

Receive Jesus Christ into your life as Saviour?

Oh, yes.

Let me say one other thing. I'll say it very plainly. When Christ comes into a life as **Saviour** He comes to do something for you: **to forgive you and give you eternal life.** But, also He comes as **Lord.** He comes as **Master and King.** He comes to demand something of you. He says there is a throne room in your heart and that throne is rightly His. He made you. He redeemed you. He bought you. He says that He wants to take His rightful place on the throne of your life. **Are you willing to yield your life, to surrender your life, to Him, out of gratitude for the gift of eternal life?**

Receive Jesus Christ into your life as Lord?

Yes, I would like to.

Would you like to repent of your sins and follow Him? That means that you will turn from what you have been doing that is not pleasing to Him and follow Him as He reveals His will to you in His Word. Is this what you would like to do?

Repent of your sins?

I would like to try.

All right, Rene. **The Lord is here right now.** We can go to Him now in **prayer** and we can tell Him that **you want to cease trusting in your own strivings and you want to put your trust in Christ the Lord for your salvation and receive Him as your**

D. The prayer of commitment

personal Saviour. Is this truly what you want?

Yes.

All right. May I point out to you, Rene, that the Lord is **looking at your heart more than He is listening to your lips.** He says, "Ye shall seek Me and find Me when ye seek for Me with all of your heart." If this is really what you mean, then the Lord will hear your prayer and grant you eternal life. Let us pray.

Preparatory prayer

Father, I pray that now Thou would grant to Rene the gift of eternal life. May Thy Spirit draw her unto Thyself. Grant her **faith to believe** Thy promise. Grant her **repentance** to turn from her sins. **Reveal unto her Christ crucified** today.

Prayer together

(Heads still bowed.) Rene, the Lord said, "Where two or three are gathered together in My name there I am in the midst of them." He is right here. You are not talking to me now but to Him. If you really want eternal life will you say to Him:

Lord Jesus, I want you to come into my life right now. (She repeats each phrase). I am a sinner. I have been trusting myself and my own good works. But now I put my trust in Thee. I accept You as my own personal Saviour. I believe You died for me. I receive you as Lord and Master over my life. Help me to turn from my sins and to follow You. I accept Your gift of eternal life. I am not worthy of it but I thank You for it.

Amen.

(Continuing in prayer with heads bowed).

Assurance of pardon

Father, You have heard the prayer which Rene has prayed. And I ask that in this quiet moment Thy Holy Spirit will grant unto her the assurance of life eternal; grant unto her the certainty that her sins are forgiven. Grant that she may hear in the depths of her soul Thy voice saying, "Thy sins be forgiven thee. Go in peace." Grant, O Christ, that she may hear Thy voice saying, "As far as the east is from the west, so far have I put thy sins from thee, never to remember them against thee any more. He that believeth on Me shall not come into condemnation. He that trusteth in Me is passed from death unto life. He that believeth on Me shall never perish but has everlasting life." In Jesus' Name, we pray. Amen.

Rene, I want you to look now at what God says about what you have just done. In **John 6:47** the Lord says something very significant. I would like you to read this. "Verily, verily, I say unto you, he that believeth in Me hath everlasting life." All right, Rene, in our prayer you didn't hear any angel choirs; heaven didn't open. However, by a simple act of faith you have put your trust in Jesus Christ for your salvation. Did you mean that?

E. The assurance of salvation

Yes, I did.

Who are you now trusting, Rene, for your salvation?

Jesus Christ.

He says, he that believeth, that is, he that trusteth in Me—that doesn't mean an intellectual assent for you have believed in Christ all your life. This doesn't mean trusting Him for temporal affairs. You've done that all your life. **Saving faith means trusting Christ alone for eternal salvation.** This is what you have done today. Jesus says that you have everlasting life. Do you believe Him?

Yes, I do.

Rene, if you should die in your sleep tonight, where would you wake up?

In heaven.

God said it. That settles it. **Praise the Lord! Welcome, Rene, to the family of God.**

The rejoicing of angels!

55

AN ANALYSIS OF THE PRESENTATION

During the time of the **Introduction,** the mood needs to be somewhat light. Often those you visit are rigid in the initial moments and hardly respond to you. Humor at this point can cause them to relax and change their whole attitude. Some visit as if they were "friendly undertakers" who have arrived to dispose of the body!

We are trying to bridge the gap from being strangers to becoming friends. We will accomplish this by showing genuine interest in our prospects and by being aware of the situation. By being interested in their interests you show yourself as a friend. Sincere compliments about the person or his accomplishments will go far toward establishing the necessary rapport.

The purpose of this five-point Introduction is to bring about a smooth transition into the Gospel. The old way of accosting a man on the street, grabbing him by the lapels and asking, "Brother, are you saved?" is repugnant. Why?

The purpose of the Introduction

Let me illustrate. At a conference grounds recently, an elderly gentleman, evidently a Christian for many years, said to me, "Preacher, I want you to tell me what's wrong. I walked up to a group of five or six people and said to one man, 'Brother, are you ready to meet God?' "

Earn the right to ask personal questions

I said, "What happened? You're still in one piece!"

"He didn't answer me."

57

"He didn't answer you? Why?"

"That's what I want to know. Why didn't he answer me?"

"Suppose there were four or five people standing here and I said, 'Bill, tell me, how are your kidneys today?' That has some mean overtones. What right have I to walk up to you and ask you something like that?"

Is there much difference between asking a man about his kidneys and asking him about his soul? There are overtones to that also.

But given a proper set of circumstances I could say to a man, "Tell me, how is it with your kidneys today?" This would elicit neither a smile nor an embarrassment. It would bring a frank, candid answer and he would appreciate my asking the question. The necessary circumstances are: I would be a physician treating him for a kidney disorder; he has taken medicine and has come to report. I ask the question. It's very natural. He would answer, "You know, doctor, it's really better now. I'm glad to see you're really concerned."

We have files of letters from people thanking us for asking them what they were trusting in for eternal life. However, we did not hit them cold with, "Brother, are you ready to meet God?" We first established rapport. **We earned the right to ask personal questions.** A transition from the secular situation to the presentation of the Gospel took place.

Jesus' use of the "Five Laws of Selling"

There are five great Laws of Selling: Attention, Interest, Desire, Conviction and Close. Did salesmen invent these? No, they just extracted them. They learned that is the way to move people to action. This is what Jesus did, for example, with the woman at the well.

Attention

He began where she was and got her attention.

58

"Give Me to drink."

"How is it you ask me? We have nothing to do with each other."

"If you knew who was asking you for water, you would ask Me and I would give you living water." Now she was really interested.

Interest

"Where would you get living water? The well is deep and you have nothing to draw with. Are you greater than Jacob who gave us this well?"

"He that drinks of this water will thirst again, but whoever drinks of the water I give will never thirst." Now she desired ardently what Jesus offered.

Desire

"Give me this water so I will never thirst again or have to come here to draw." Here she was: a woman of ill repute, having to go to the well at noon when no one else was there. Everyone else came in the cool of the day. She seems more interested in not going to the well to draw than in not thirsting again. "Give it to me."

"Go call your husband." He put His finger on her sin. Did she have to have her husband to get saved? No. That was her sin.

Conviction

"I have no husband."

"You're right. You had five husbands and the man you live with now isn't your husband." He drove home the evidence of her sinfulness.

She tried to avoid the issue. "Our fathers worship in this mountain; you worship in that mountain; blah . . . blah . . . blah . . . . When Messiah comes He will tell us about these matters."

(Off the subject)

Jesus used something from her digression to get back on the main subject, "I that speak to you, am He."

59

The Close

Now she confronts the living Christ. She is brought to the point of decision. She must either accept or reject Him.

There you see a beautiful piece of workmanship by the Master Workman, who says we should copy Him in dealing with people. He had a smooth transition from where she was to where He wanted her to go.

Begin where prospect is

Thus we begin with a person where he is.

I. The Introduction
A. Their secular life

Upon entering the home the first thing with which you will deal is the person's secular life. This covers a lot of things. It will include the basic amenities of the day—questions about where the person is from and what he does. At this point we will do two things:

1. Ask a question that is near to the core of his life. We will not ask about something on the periphery of his interest, but we will search the room for some indication of his interest. A specially placed and lighted painting; a group of portraits of children; trophies from golf, swimming or bowling all furnish materials for saying, "Tell me something about yourself." After asking this, **be quiet and listen to him talk for five minutes.** People usually are most interested in what they themselves have to say.

2. Then you will **pay him a sincere compliment.** In order to do this you will have had to listen to what he was saying.

B. Their church

You are visiting from the church. It is natural for you to talk about his previous church experiences. At this point you will begin to qualify the person. Whom do you have—a "Pharisee," a "Sadducee," or a libertine? You learn more about the person, how he views the church, and what

60

his relationship was to the church back home. DON'T CRITICIZE his denomination, his congregation, his minister, or him as a person. Keep in mind that you go to make a friendly visit and to show your interest and concern for him.

It is logical to move from discussing his previous church activity into the fact of his visit to your church. Find out if his impression is negative or positive, hostile or friendly. It will be helpful at this point if your service was meaningful and encouraging to him. Ask him if he noted any unique aspects of your worship and your people. The best preparation for an evangelistic call is a vital worship service for the visitors and a friendly, helpful congregation to greet the visitors and assist them in finding the nursery, rest rooms, etc., according to their needs.

C. Our church

The testimony may take either of two forms. It may be a personal testimony (either your own or that of another), **or it may be a church testimony.** In the accompanying presentation, a church testimony is used in order to establish the mission of the church: i.e., to proclaim the Gospel that men and women may have eternal life. (To see how a personal testimony might be used, see "Giving a Personal Testimony" in the Testimony chapter.)

D. Testimony

1. This question brings the person to the point of saying, in effect, "I don't have eternal life. I would like to know how to have it. Will you please share it with me?" We always want to find out if the person already has eternal life.

E. Two Questions

I. "Have you come to a place in your spiritual experience where you know you have eternal life?"

Suppose you were selling an encyclopedia and you spent two hours in a home presenting a family with the wonderful advantages of owning the Britannica. Then you would ask them what they think of it. The father turns and says, "It's marvelous. In fact, I thinks it's so wonderful that I bought a set six months ago and it's in the next room."

No encyclopedia salesman would be that stupid!

Yet many who are witnessing for Christ make this very mistake. They do not learn if the person has eternal life already. After presenting the Gospel they hear these lovely words: "Oh, yes. I've always believed that."

Most people will say they are not certain that they have eternal life. If one says, "I know I have eternal life," you must then determine on what he is basing that hope and distinguish true assurance from presumption. The Westminster Confession of Faith points out that " . . hypocrites, and other unregenerate men, may vainly deceive themselves . . . of being in the . . . estate of salvation; which hope of theirs shall perish." Dr. McDowell Richards, president of Columbia Theological Seminary, said one day, "Assurance is having a confidence of eternal life which is rested upon the sure foundation of Jesus Christ, but presumption is presuming ourselves to have eternal life when in fact our confidence is based on nothing more than the flimsy foundation of our own self-righteousness."

2. "Suppose you were to die tonight and stand before God, and He were to ask you, 'Why should I let you into My heaven?' What would you say?"

2. **The second question enables us to discern upon what foundation one is trusting for eternal life.** Why do we ask, "Why should God let you into heaven?" rather than, "What must I do to be saved?" The latter is a biblical question that has a biblical answer. One who has gone to Sunday school and has some acquaintance with the Scriptures will respond like a computer. Feed such a person the question in biblical language and he will push a mental button, the machine will whirl and hum and out comes the right answer: "Believe on the

Lord Jesus Christ, and thou shalt be saved and thy house." This may be his sincere faith, or merely a parrot reply devoid of true understanding. You will have no way of knowing which.

In asking the question, "Why should God let you into heaven?" we feed a question that has not been programmed. There is no rote—no automatically learned—answer. Also it is a neutral question, i.e., it does not lead the person to give a presupposed answer. From the answer given, you then know what the person is truly trusting for eternal life. It's helpful at this point to rephrase the answer: "Let me see if I understand you. You would say to God . . ." **and then repeat what he has just told you. This will preclude his saying at the end,** "Oh, I've always believed in Jesus Christ and trusted Him alone for salvation."

Often when you ask a person, "Why should God let you into heaven?" you will get an answer something like, "Well, I don't know." **Is there some way to get an answer that will let you know what he is trusting? Here are several methods we have found effective.**

How to get an answer

1. Much like a football player, you have "hit the line" and can't get through. You need to back up, gain a bit more speed and hit it again in a bit different manner. You will **stress the significance and importance of the question.** "That's really a thought-provoking question, isn't it? When I first heard it I was no theologian but I did have enough sense to realize that it's truly a significant question, isn't it? I came to realize that it's the most important question in the world. If I could not give God the right answer I would miss heaven. And the other option isn't too pleasant to think about. I figured that was really a question I needed to know the answer to. I realized Jesus had said, 'What shall it profit a man if he gain the whole world and lose his own soul?' I know you don't have a theological dissertation pre-

Change the wording

pared on the subject, but just offhand, what comes to your mind? What do you think you would say if you had to face God and He asked you, 'Why should I let you into my heaven'?''

Your prospect will find it harder to say again, "I don't know." You have discussed that this is really an important question—the most important question in the world according to your authority, Jesus Christ! Also, you have taken the edge off the situation by pointing out that you do not expect him to have a theological dissertation on the subject. **Finally, you have changed the wording from, "What would you say?" to "What do you think you would say?"**

Make the question general

2. In the event your prospect gives another, "I don't know," or "It's hard to say," you still want to get an answer. You will now want to change from a personal question to a general one.

"Well, I sort of felt the same way. That's a difficult question to answer. But may I ask you a different question? As much as you've been going to church all your life, I'm sure you have gathered some idea as to what the entrance requirements to heaven are. I would be interested in what a man of your experience would say God requires of any person who would enter heaven."

If this elicits a suitable response you then may add, "Now, I suppose that since we have had time to look at it, these are really the things upon which you yourself are basing your hope of getting into heaven, aren't they?"

In this case you have made it more difficult to plead ignorance. You have reminded your prospect that he's been sitting in church for years. He's not going to admit: "I'm so stupid I have not learned a thing! I just sat there sleeping!" Also, the question is no longer right on him—

not, "What would you say?" but "What are the entrance requirements?"—in general for anyone.

3. However, **what if he still is evasive and doesn't know?** You might do this, but only as a last resort. "Well, here's what I thought. You have to keep the Golden Rule and live by the Ten Commandments, be a good citizen and neighbor and not hurt anyone intentionally. Are these the ideas that have been going around in your mind?"

Tell what your answer was

Here you are on the dangerous ground of putting out words for him to claim as his own. This tends to be leading. The only reason for using this approach is that by this time your prospect has given good evidence that he is not trusting Christ and probably is trusting some form of good works but has not been able to verbalize it.

4. **If there is still no answer,** or if again he acknowledges that he does not know what he would say, you can now nail him down with, **"Then you just really don't know how to get into heaven, do you?**

Agree that he doesn't know

"You're sort of like the man in Jesus' story. The king came to him and said, 'Friend, how camest thou in hither?' Do you know what he said? He said the same thing you said! He was speechless! He really didn't know what to say. Do you know what happened to him? The servants bound him and cast him into outer darkness. Now, we don't want that to happen to you, do we?

"Do you remember the "$64,000 Question" that used to be on TV? If a contestant gave the wrong answer he would be told, 'Step down.' And you know, the same thing happened if he gave no answer. There are some situations like that in life where you have to answer, where a wrong answer and no answer are the same thing. It's a long way to step down from God. And we don't want you to have to do that. **Would you like me to share with you what the biblical answer to that question is?"**

By this time you have come far from the front door. As the door opened you were strangers. Now your prospect knows you as one interested in him, his background and his opinions. He also knows you are knowledgeable in the spiritual realm. You know a great deal about him. You know his interest in the church, his attitude towards our church, his view of himself, and most important, his eternal destiny as of this moment. If he is lost, you hope by God's grace that his destiny will change within the next hour or two. You are now ready to present the facts of the Gospel.

II. The Gospel itself

In the Introduction you have found out what the person is trusting for salvation. Equally important, he has found out. Until you helped him clarify it, he probably wasn't aware of what he was trusting for eternal life. We begin now to tear down this foundation which is inadequate. Now we are about to show the product and show the prospect that he needs it. Remember, you put the value on your product by the way you speak about it. It will seem as valuable to your prospect as it does to you. Think about what you are saying. Talk about God's Good News in a manner befitting the greatest story ever told! The expression on your face may be far more important than the words on your lips. Start thinking about heaven before talking about it!

Beware of your attitude at this point lest you convey: "Would you like ME (wise guy) to tell YOU (stupid) how you can get smart (like I am)." In other words, avoid talking down to people. People who have been going to Sunday school classes and worship services know a lot of facts that form a spiritual jigsaw puzzle. Each Sunday they get another piece or two to put in the box. This week they got a sermon about the Good Samaritan. That was nice. Into the box it goes. Occasionally they shake all the pieces around but they don't seem to fall together. Christianity seems to be just a large number of pieces floating through the air. Noah, David and Goliath, the Tower of Babel, Jesus healing a blind man, and a little man up in a tree—isolated stories without much meaning and with no interrelationship. A few pieces are missing. These we supply as we present the Gospel. These key pieces enable everything else to fall into place.

The things in this Presentation that most people don't know are:

1. Man cannot save himself
2. God is holy and just and must punish sin
3. Christ is God
4. His death on the cross was for our sins
5. He offers heaven as a gift
6. The meaning of grace
7. The meaning of faith

These are the points we must emphasize. To verbally underscore them you must stop and say these key points deliberately. You dare not go through the whole Gospel at the same pace and in the same tone of voice, or finally your host will say, "That's very interesting. It's time to go to bed. I can hardly keep my eyes open." Charles Spurgeon says if you gently rock the cradle and put them to sleep, all you have to do is give the cradle a good jerk and the babies wake up!

Usually you will not have to go through most of the above, for you will get an answer to your question on the first or second attempt. The problem then arises as to how to deal with the wrong answer that they have given you. Let me share a word of my own experience over the years in dealing with this problem in the hope that you may avoid some of the mistakes I have made. I

How to deal with their wrong answer

67

began by answering the question directly: "No, that is not correct, Mr. Jones. The answer the Bible gives is quite different from your answer." The problem I ran into here should be obvious. **Someone has said that the most pleasant words in the English language are "You were right," which would seeem to indicate that some of the most unpleasant words are "You were wrong."** These words tended to raise the hackles on my prospect's neck and I often found myself engaged in an argument right at the outset. I won a number of arguments and lost a great many prospects. Finally I decided to try a different tack. Instead of telling them from the outset that their answer was wrong, I said that their answer was interesting but that it raised a number of questions. And then I went into the Gospel and waited until the end of the Gospel presentation to tell them that they had been wrong. However, I now discovered a new problem. Since some time had elapsed since they had given their answer I found that many people would now try to wiggle out of their answer or else deny that they had ever said it. So I found myself right back where I started.

After a good many years of struggling with this problem, I was led by the Lord to a solution. I had thought that there must be a way to tell them from the outset that they were wrong and yet make them happy to hear it. I am happy to say there is a way that this can be done. We now respond to their wrong answer something like this: "You know, Mr. Jones, when you answered that first question ('Do you know for sure you have eternal life?') I thought that I had some good news for you. But after hearing your answer to this second question ('Why should God let you into heaven?') I know that I have some good news for you. In fact, I would go so far as to say that in the next two minutes you are going to hear the greatest good news that you have ever heard in your entire life! That's quite a statement, isn't it? Well, let's see if I can back it up. All my life I thought just what you said—if ever I were to get to heaven

I would have to earn, deserve, or merit it. And then I discovered the most wonderful thing in the world—that according to the Bible heaven, eternal life, is absolutely a free gift. Isn't that amazing?"

This should be said with great enthusiasm and exuberance. I have found that usually will produce an enthusiastic and open response on the part of the listener. This is due to a number of factors: (1) it is such tremendous good news; (3) it is almost universally unknown by the unregenerate person; (3) the shock effect of hearing the most unexpected news right at the beginning; (4) and very importantly, the enthusiastic and exuberant manner in which the Good News is told precludes a hostile reaction.

Most people know that they are sinners even though they may not realize the seriousness of that accusation. Many times they have heard, "All have sinned." So they conclude that sin is something everyone is doing, therefore it cannot be so bad. "Oh, yes, I'm a sinner. But not so bad a sinner that I can't go to heaven by being reasonably good." They don't know that because they are sinners and God's standard is perfection they cannot qualify for heaven. Here we must clear the deck. The Scripture says to tear down and to build up. We have to tear away, clear away, the old foundation on which they build their hope of eternal life before we can build up. In telling a man that he is a sinner and cannot save himself you simply show him that what he has told you will not work. By showing him what the standard is and that he has fallen short of the standard, you convey the idea that he needs the product you are offering.

It is good at the end of Point 1 to show that what he is trusting is inadequate—that no one could get to heaven on that basis. You might say, "You understand that because God's standard is perfection, and none of us have come up to it, it is impossible for anyone to get to heaven by

**Man cannot
save himself**

69

doing enough good things?" His reply would be, "Yes, I do." Now your prospect has reaffirmed that you not only understood him correctly and knew what he meant when he answered the question as to why God should let him into heaven, but now he sees that what he meant is an impossibility. The reason this is a good place to do this is that you have not given him anything to substitute for it yet. After you have given him the right answer he might say, "Oh, no! I didn't mean that! I meant this—what you just said." But by the end of Point 1 you haven't given the right answer. All you have done is taken away what he was trusting in formerly.

Occasionally one will disagree with you and say, "No, that's not what I meant." He realizes that he may have shown what he's trusting in is wrong. He may not want to admit this. Your reply in such a situation is, "Wonderful! I'm glad that I found this out now for I thought that's what you meant. Tell me, what did you mean?" Thus you can get another commitment from him at this point. All he is going to do is point to some other part of himself. Then you can continue with the Gospel.

God is just, and must punish sin

The nature of God is an element left out of many presentations of the Gospel. To leave it out, especially in the present day, deprives the Gospel of much of its meaning. Perhaps 200 years ago most people had valid conceptions of God. This is not true today. Ultimately all theological heresy is caused by a misconception of the nature of God. When we fail to understand His nature we cannot understand His Gospel. Many church people hold a Christian Science concept of God as merely love. If this is one's view of God, he will fit all you say as you present the Gospel into that mold and it will be meaningless to him. God is love—so what if man is a sinner? God is love—so what if Christ died? God is love—so why worry whether everyone believes in Him if everyone will be saved anyway?

70

A good argument could be made that the second commandment is the one most frequently broken today: "Thou shalt not make unto thee any graven images." You may have heard the story of two servicemen who returned to base on Saturday night after a week's leave. They had lived it up wildly during the week and had done everything a serviceman could do on leave. On Sunday morning they went to chapel to find the chaplain preaching on the Ten Commandments. As they were slinking out the door after service, one was heard to say to the other, "Well, at least I ain't made no graven images lately!" But the problem with all he had done, basically, was involved with the fact that he started with a graven image—not made of wood or stone but conjured in the factory of his mind! Men create gods in their own image.

One time I was reading to a lady what God said He would do to the guilty. She said, "Oh, my God would never do that!" I said, "Madam, you are right. Your god would never do that. The problem is, your god doesn't exist except in your own mind. You have created a god in your own image, according to your own liking, and now you have fallen down and worshiped him. This is idolatry."

This is one of the most prevalent sins of our day. How often have you heard it said, "God would never do that!" What God wouldn't do it? The God of the Bible? He says a thousand times exactly what He will do. If one says God wouldn't do these things, he is speaking of the god he has made up: a false god.

Therefore, in a time with this heresy so prevalent, we need to **stress the true nature of God**—that He is not only loving and kind and merciful, but that He is also holy and cannot condone sin. He is also righteous and has promised to punish sin and visit our iniquity with stripes. It is the nature

71

of God that makes the whole concept of Christ's Person and work meaningful.

Christ is God

In our society people know many facts about Jesus of Nazareth, but they do not know He is divine. When they hear "Jesus is the Son of God," they have some faulty understanding. Perhaps they believe He is only different in degree from every human being. "Are we not all the sons of God?" they ask. They do not see anything unique about Jesus except He was more successful than we in keeping God's Law and He was a brilliant teacher. For others, the claim that Jesus was the Son of God means that He was more than a man, but they believe He was less than God. In other words, He was God and man mingled in one nature so He is seen as a superhuman being but not as a fully divine being. We must underscore the truth that the Babe of Bethlehem's manger was none other than the Word of creation, the mighty God who created and sustains heaven and earth and all things.

His death on the cross was for our sins

Nearly everyone we meet knows that Jesus died on the cross of Calvary. Hardly anyone is aware of the significance of that death according to the teaching of the Scriptures. The death of Christ has no meaning for a man until the concept of imputation grasps his soul as it did Luther's. One must see that his sins were laid to Christ. He must realize that Christ assumed our guilt. As Paul put it, God made Christ to be sin for us that we might be made the righteousness of God in Him. The cross has meaning for a man when he knows that his guilt was imputed to the Son by the Father; and when he knows, further, that the Father laid upon the Son the hell that every sinner deserves. **Let a man see his sin laid on Christ on the cross and then that cross has meaning for him.**

He offers heaven as a gift

Making this statement just once does not deal with the point. Every religion in the world teaches that man must earn the favor of God by doing something. He must qualify himself. He must make himself worthy of God's gifts. In contrast, Christianity proclaims that God's favor, His blessings, and heaven itself can be had only as free gifts. You cannot obliterate the non-Christian concept of making oneself worthy of God's favor with the contrary statement said once. Say it 20 times in different ways! "Heaven is free! Eternal life is God's gift to you. His favor is given graciously. You do not—you cannot earn your way to heaven. Never can you deserve to dwell with the holy, sin-hating One." After all this, MAYBE he will understand—maybe he won't. **Pray that God graciously will open the ears of your prospect and give him understanding!**

Everyone seemingly has heard of "grace." Perhaps it is the most frequently used concept in Christian cricles. Tragically, however, few can tell you what grace means. The non-Christian adage, "God helps those who help themselves," is deeply embedded in the American mind. Because our ancestors dug and clawed a nation out of the wilderness, the American traditionally wants to stand on his own two feet. He feels he must carry his share of the load, all of which is commendable. However, if this spirit carries over into an understanding of grace it can be eternally fatal.

God has revealed Himself as "the Help of the helpless." So long as he thinks he must contribute his own efforts to the work of God, your prospect does not understand his true condition or the work of Christ. He does not realize that sin has incapacitated him so that he cannot do anything meritorious in God's sight. Neither does he know the sufficiency of Christ's sacrifice. By adding his supposed goodness to the work of our Lord, he says he believes Christ's work to be insufficient.

Paul's teaching in Romans 11 is that grace and works are mutually exclusive. "If it is of grace, then is it no more of works: otherwise grace is no more grace. But if it be of works, then is it no

The meaning of grace

73

more grace: otherwise work is no more work."
This must be communicated to your prospect if he is to make a good profession. For salvation your prospect may be trusting wholly in Christ, wholly in self, or partially in Christ and partially in self. Many unsaved who are related to the church fall into the latter category. However, that position is essentially the same as trusting fully in self. "Assuming that Christ has done His part sufficiently, if I am to be saved I must do my part acceptably. If, on the other hand, I am lost, it must be because I did not do enough to win God's favor." Thus is the logic of partial trust in Christ and partial trust in self. As one has said, "Grace is not the thread of gold decorating the garment, rather, like the ancient mercy seat, gold, pure gold through and through."

The meaning of faith

This, too, is crucial, for this is the point of personal appropriation of eternal life. John Calvin said that the Roman Catholic church taught him the deity of Christ, the Trinity, the atonement; but the one thing the church did not teach him was how to appropriate the atonement for himself. Even today there are those who know all of the doctrines of the faith but they don't know how to get eternal life for themselves. Their problem: an inadequate or false concept of saving faith.

One has rightly pointed out that there are **three elements to saving faith: knowledge, assent, and trust.** We may know about something without giving assent to it. For example, one cult teaches that Christ is incarnate today in a man in India. I know about this but I do not assent to it. Similarly, one may have a knowledge that the Bible teaches that man is a sinner who cannot save himself, without assenting to the truth of this statement. Thus to knowledge must be added assent to the facts of our historic faith. However, one can know about, and assent to, many historical facts without trusting them. We know about Alexander the Great and assent to the historical

74

record concerning his conquests. Further, we assent to the fact that he was a military genius. However, I hope no one is trusting Alexander to do anything for him! That would be rather ludicrous. Added to knowledge and assent is what Luther termed "fiducia": **trust.**

As you present the Gospel, keeping the note of "What are you trusting in for salvation?" you can effectively illustrate the meaning of saving faith with the use of **an empty chair.** Let that chair represent the Lord Jesus. Your prospect knows it is a chair. He believes (assents) that the chair will hold him off the floor, provide comfort to his body and relax his weary spirit. But it's not doing any of these things for him for one obvious reason: he's not sitting in it. Neither is that chair of any benefit to you for the same reason. Now the chair in which you are sitting can represent all you once trusted for eternal life. Point out that this is inadequate to your needs and would let you fall into hell. **By actually moving from the "chair of your own good works" to the "chair of Jesus Christ" you visually and verbally illustrate the meaning of trusting Christ alone for salvation.** Just as you no longer are in "the chair of your good works" but in "the chair of Jesus Christ," so you have transferred your trust for eternal life from yourself to the Lord.

A more subtle substitute for saving faith is trusting the Lord for temporal well-being while trusting self for eternal life. Some have difficulty making this distinction but the distinction is necessary. It spells the difference between heaven and hell!

We can consider Luther. Before his conversion he was not an agnostic, skeptic or atheist. He believed in God. While in the monastery he undoubtedly trusted God for some things. When he made the pilgrimage to Rome, did he not trust the Lord for safety, lodging and meals, and health? Certainly! Similarly, John Wesley trusted the Lord to take him safely from England to his mission post in the New World. All the while these men were trusting themselves for a successful journey from earth to heaven! They knew about, and trusted in, transportation by faith, long before they knew and trusted justification by faith.

You can use "the chair of Jesus Christ" to illustrate the concept of trusting Him for temporal matters. As you restate your prospect was trusting God for health, you can place a pen on "the chair of Jesus Christ." Trusting Him for travel mercies can be represented by a key ring. A billfold will indicate trust in God for financial needs. All the while the prospect himself is still sitting in "the chair of his own good works." He is still trusting himself for the eternal well-being of his soul.

III. The Commitment
A. The qualifying Question: "Does this make sense to you?"

Many people are afraid to ask for a commitment when they finish presenting the Gospel because they do not know whether they have brought the person with them or have lost them somewhere along the way. **The qualifying question which is "Does this make sense to you?" will elicit a response which is either positive or negative.** A positive response will be something of this sort: "Oh, yes, that is wonderful! Why didn't I hear it before?" etc. A negative response will be something like: "Well, that is very complicated. I will have to give this a lot of thought. I'm not sure . . . "

What to do: If the response is positive you know that the person is with you and you are ready to ask the commitment question. If the response is uncertain then go back to the beginning and quickly review the main points of the Gospel, asking as you go, "Do you understand this point, 'Man is a sinner'?" etc.

It is important to know exactly how you are going to ask for the commitment and even what words you are going to use. For the inexperienced, this is a tense moment and the commitment question should be thoroughly learned. This will help the novice through his anxiety. This question is chosen for two reasons:

1. By it you are coming out of the Gospel at the same place that you went in. That is, you began your presentation by asking them if they would like for you to share with them how they could have eternal life. Having done that and having ascertained that they have understood, you are now asking them if they would like to receive this eternal life.

2. You are asking for your initial commitment at the most positive point possible. "Would you like to receive the free gift of eternal life?" This is obviously a better place to begin than some such question as, "Would you like to crucify your old nature?"

One danger at the point of closing is that the novice fears to ask for a commitment. Therefore, to overcome that hesitancy to close, we have endeavored to make this as simple and as pleasant as possible.

However, another danger at the point of closing is a premature commitment—a commitment which is not based on a thorough understanding of what is involved in accepting Christ as Saviour and Lord. Therefore, at this point we recommend clarification. This would involve essentially the questions found in the Commitment section of the Presentation. These questions involve an elaboration of the meaning of faith. The emphasis to be given at this point will depend upon the attitude of the person to whom you are speaking. If he is evidently repentant and moved, perhaps even to tears as occasionally has been the case, then this need not be belabored. If, however, the person seems to be thinking that he just might get in on a good deal without its affecting his life, then the aspect of repentance and the Lordship of Christ should be heavily emphasized.

B. **The commitment Question: "Would you like to receive the gift of eternal life which Christ is offering to you?"**

C. **The clarification of the commitment**

77

D. The prayer of commitment

Many have been lost at this point because of the way in which they were asked to pray. It is especially true of adults and older people who have perhaps been in church for many years and should know how to pray but have never prayed in their lives. They are horrified at the thought of having to pray spontaneously in front of a stranger. Therefore, in asking them to pray, I have found this wording very helpful: (note especially the pronouns)

"Well, Rene, if this is really what **you** want we can go to the Lord in prayer right where we are. **I** can lead **us** in prayer and **we** will tell Him what you have told me just now—you want Christ to come into your heart to be your Saviour and Lord and you want to repent of your sins and receive the gift of eternal life. Is this **really** what you want, Rene?"

"Yes, it is."

"All right, then, let us bow our heads in prayer."

In the prayer itself I recommend three parts which are helpful:

1. **Pray for him:** that God would give him faith and repentance.

2. **Pray with him:** in the actual commitment almost any statement from the Gospel outline is appropriate here, allowing him to repeat it after you.

3. **Pray for him:** that the Holy Spirit will grant him assurance. Give the Spirit of God some time to seal these things to his heart (an example of such prayer is at the end of the printed Presentation).

E. The assurance of salvation

At this point it is important to point him to the promises of God and to help him take hold of them by faith. A very simple and forthright promise is

78

John 6:47 which we almost always use. After the prayer the witness might say something like this:

"Rene, that was the most important prayer that you ever prayed and the most important decision that you have ever made. I would like to show you what Christ has to say about what you have just done."

(Open your New Testament and let her read aloud John 6:47.) After she reads it, say,

"Hold that place for a moment and let us analyze that carefully. It is Christ the Son of God, the King of the Kingdom, who is speaking. He says, 'Truthfully, truthfully, I say unto you, he that believeth on Me—and we have shown that this is not merely an intellectual assent (you have had that all your life)—but he that trusteth upon Me alone for salvation, he that resteth upon Me for eternal life, hath (that is Old English for 'has')—a present possession—eternal life.' By the way, eternal life in the Bible always means 'in heaven.' (Some people think that eternal life merely means a continued existence somewhere, somehow.)

"Now, Rene, you just told Christ in your prayer that you now trust in Him alone for your salvation. As best you know your heart, Rene, did you really mean that?"

"Yes."

"Well, Rene, do you believe that Jesus Christ meant what He said in this promise you just read?"

"I do."

"Then let me ask you this question: If you died tonight in your sleep—and you just might!—where would you wake up?"

"In heaven."

"Who said so?"

"Jesus Christ."

(Reaching over and shaking her hand . . .)

"Let me welcome you, Rene, to the Kingdom of God."

THE PROPER USE
OF TESTIMONY

If a Christian is to be an effective witness for his Saviour, the first tool he needs is a clear, forceful personal testimony. If you have met God in Jesus Christ in your own life, you have found God working according to His promises. Your experience of God's faithfulness is the substance of your testimony. As you prepare your testimony, realize you are fashioning an evangelistic tool so you will be a more proficient witness.

A tool for evangelism

Some Christians give admirable testimonies—testimonies with zip and life—testimonies devoid of rough spots and trite platitudes. However, others stumble and bumble in a disorganized, uninteresting, ineffectual manner. We must sharpen our tools and learn to use them effectively.

Giving a personal testimony is the first aspect of witnessing—simply telling what Jesus Christ has meant to you. When Jesus healed the demoniac in Gadara, He said, "Go home to thy friends, and tell them how great things the Lord hath done for thee, and hath had compassion on thee." Now, if you cannot tell someone that Christ has saved you, you are not an evangelist; you are an evangelistic field and you need an evangelist to lead you to conversion. This is not to say that you must know **when** you were converted. However, you must know **if** you have been converted. Many people don't know when they became Christians. One of the great preachers of our generation, Dr. Peter Eldersveld, said that he could remember clearly when he was three years old, and he knew that at that time he trusted in the blood of Jesus Christ alone for his salvation. He was well taught by his parents, and came to a very early faith and could remember nothing else. **In order to witness for Christ you must have the assurance that you have eternal life and that Christ Jesus is your Saviour.**

Three times in the Book of Acts, Paul gives his personal testimony. If we study these accounts we will discover the three essential elements are:

1. What I was before I became a Christian.
2. How I became a Christian.
3. What Jesus Christ has meant in my life.

A. A Positive Emphasis

Emphasize the positive

One of the common errors in giving a testimony is to belabor the first point and minimize the third. Just the opposite should be our method. You do not help the people by giving them a tedious life history. They have no particular interest in where you attended school, where your parents live, or when you moved from here to there. Rather, do as Jesus commanded the demoniac: "Go . . . and tell how great things the Lord hath done for thee." **Emphasize the positive benefits.**

I remember one Christian who accompanied me on an evangelistic call. In response to my request that he give a testimony, he said, "When I accepted Christ, I lost all my friends. They wouldn't have anything to do with me. Then I lost my job. You know, all the people who do worldly things (and he mentioned half a dozen things that evidently thrilled the people we were visiting) give you up when you give up these worldly practices." It was as if he had given a five minute discourse on why one should not become a Christian! Suppose you saw a cigarette ad that showed an emaciated man, his countenance manifesting excruciating pain, and he said to you, "Smoke my

82

brand of cigarettes. It will help you develop cancer more quickly. You can have less wind if you join us. And your hair will smell worse!'' Such an ad would not convince you to buy their brand! It seems that many Christians are about that effective when they tell why a person ought to become a Christian. **Emphasize the positive benefits of being a Christian.**

Let us now consider the parts of a testimony and see how each can be made meaningful to others.

What I was before

Here you either encourage people to "tune you out" or to sit up and listen carefully to what you are saying. At this point you are making an effort to identify with your prospect, and have him identify with you.

Identify with your prospect

In the conversation concerning their secular life and church background, you have gained enough insight to determine whether your prospect is self-righteous, a libertine, an agnostic, indifferent, etc. In telling him what you were before Christ, **select truthful statements about yourself that will enable him to see himself in your life.** For example, you discover your prospect to be a self-righteous intellectual who is caring for his elderly parents. You would make a fatal mistake by saying, "My parents did not do right by me. They did not give me any religious instruction, and their reprobate lives led me to become a wretched character. I embezzled my employer's funds and was unfaithful to my wife. Then I met Christ." Your prospect would think, "Good, you needed Him, but I don't!" And he would start watching his silverware in case you had a spiritual relapse.

How much better to say to your pharisaical philosopher: "I never gave any thought to the reason I was here in the world until one day such and such happened. Oh, I knew there was a heaven, but I never gave much thought about how I could get there." It does no good to tell a very righteous person what a great criminal you were, but, rather, just the aspects of your life that were similar to the life of your prospect. You thereby let him know that you were the same as he is. Then when you found something very vital that was missing from your life, he will sense something is lacking in his life.

How I became a Christian

Do not give answers before you ask the questions

As we present the Gospel, it should have certain elements of mystery. You confront the prospect with a problem in a manner that identifies him with the problem. As you let him see and feel the problem, the suspense mounts and he gets into the problem; then you solve the problem by presenting Christ in the Gospel. However, **you do not want to give any answers to questions you will ask later.**

Suppose you were witnessing to John, and Barbara is your companion on the visit. Before you establish what John is trusting for his salvation, you ask Barbara to give her testimony. She says, "The pastor came to see me and asked me why I thought I should go to heaven. I didn't know I needed to trust only in Christ, so I told him I hoped I was good enough to get in. I went to church every Sunday, and helped needy people at Christmas, and never intentionally hurt anyone. But Pastor told me I could never get to heaven that way because I was a sinner and needed the cleansing blood of Jesus Christ. So I stopped trusting what I was doing, and started trusting Christ's work on the cross for me."

Now you turn to John and ask, "John, what are you trusting for eternal life?" His certain reply will be, "I am trusting in the blood of Christ." He may not have the slightest idea about why Christ's blood avails for anything, or what is involved in the act of trusting Him for salvation. **He is just parroting the "right answer" he heard Barbara give in her testimony.**

If the testimony is used during the Introduction of the Gospel (see Outline), **speak in general terms as you tell how you became a Christian. If, how-**

ever, the testimony is all you have time for, you must make especially clear just how you passed from death unto life.

B. Motives for Becoming a Christian

Here you must not generalize or you will lose your audience. To be effective, you must be specific. You can say, "It is wonderful!" What exactly is wonderful? Or you may say, "I have peace." Exactly what do you mean? In what way do you have peace? **Be specific—make your testimony concrete.**

"It is wonderful to know when I lay my head on my pillow tonight that if I do not awaken in bed in the morning, I will awaken in paradise with God."

"I have a Christian son in Vietnam, yet my heart is filled with peace because I know he has eternal life. Even though he may be killed by an enemy mortar, he has a home awaiting him in heaven, and one day we'll be reunited there."

People remember specifics. They forget generalities. What are some points we might make in sharing what Christ means to us?

1. **He provides us with Christian fellowship and friends.** Why do unsaved people attend church? What are they looking for? How do they rate a church? The answer: **friendliness.** Friendliness is significant to people because they are lonely. A basic human need is that of friendship. When people hear that Christ creates a fellowship, they find this meaningful.

2. **He fills us with His love.** Our homes in America have every luxury conceivable. However, many lack the essential ingredient of love. Strife and jealousy lurk in gadget-filled rooms, and many marriages are little better than an armed truce. People long to be loved. A testimony to the love that Christ brings into a life and a home

What Jesus Christ has meant in my life

Be specific

What does Christ mean in the Christian's life?

Fellowship

Love

may awaken your prospect to a need that has not been met for years.

Forgiveness

3. **He forgives us and relieves us of our sense of guilt.** A major problem with which people are unable to cope is guilt. Guilt fills our psychiatric hospitals, for it fractures the human personality. It causes anxiety and depression. It creates havoc in the human heart. The greatest picture of relief from guilt is in Bunyan's allegory. As Christian kneels at the cross, the burden of guilt falls off and rolls into the empty tomb, never to be seen again. The burden of guilt is lifted at Calvary.

A Friend in my trouble

4. **Christ is Himself a Friend to lean upon in trouble**—sometimes. He imparts strength to the discouraged and worn down, to the beat. It has been charged that Christ is a crutch. How do you answer that? "That's fine. I'm a cripple. I need a crutch."

Adoption

5. **He adopts us into His family.** "He sets the solitary in families." God becomes our Father and we become brothers and sisters in Christ. Frequently we can say to a person who has just accepted Christ, "Welcome into the family of God. I have just discovered something. We are related. You and I are brothers and sisters, and we are members of the greatest family on earth: God's family."

New perspectives

6. **He gives a whole new perspective on life.** One of the most devastating questions you can ask anybody is "What are you living for?" Most people have no idea. When one becomes a Christian, all this is changed. We are given a clarity and perspective unknowable by the non-Christian. The enigmas of the universe, the questions that perplex people begin to fall into place, and we begin to see the puzzle of life more clearly.

Freedom from fear

7. **He delivers from the fears of living and dying.**

Many people are fearful. Some will say they are not afraid of hell. But they are afraid to take the garbage out at night.

C. Write It Out First

In the light of the preceding discussion, you will find it profitable to write out your own testimony. As you prepare your testimony, bear the following in mind:

1. **Avoid clichés that are meaningless to the non-Christian.**

   These jangle unbelieving ears. For example: "Receive Christ and you'll receive a blessing." This is so common to us, but the non-Christian will cringe at the thought of receiving a blessing. What is it to receive a blessing? How does it come? by mail? or does it fall from the sky? We must always distinguish the connotation from the denotation of a word. The denotation is what the word actually means according to Webster or a theological dictionary. For example, the word "evangelism" is undoubtedly, by derivation, one of the most beautiful words in our language. It comes from the word "evangel"; in turn it comes from "good angel," and it is the glad tidings. Nothing could be more beautiful.

   However, what does evangelism connote to some people? It stirs up images of Elmer Gantry and people on street corners beating drums and shouting, and doing all sorts of things unpleasant to them. The connotations of the word are the barnacles it picks up as it sails the sea of life.

   Avoid cliches

2. **Avoid giving a travelogue dealing with externals and missing the spiritual matters.**

   No travelogue

3. **Avoid vague generalities that are meaningless.**

   Avoid generalities

4. **Avoid answering questions you intend to ask later.**

   Don't give away the mystery

Avoid frivolity

5. **Avoid a frivolous attitude towards the Gospel.**

Use humor

6. **Use humor constructively.** If the situation becomes tense, you can relieve his rage by saying something funny.

Identify

7. **Identify with your prospect.**

Use quotations

8. **Use direct and indirect quotations to arouse interest.**

Speak pictorially

9. Speak pictorially. "I was in bed, and the Gospel came on the clock radio. Fortunately it was out of my reach, so I couldn't just roll over and turn it off. I got out of bed and just about the time I got to the radio . . . " Here is a situation that people can visualize. If they are not seeing in their minds the thing you are talking about, they are probably seeing something that they are thinking about, rather than listening to you.

Sharpen your tools

Now you can shape, sharpen, smooth and perfect your personal testimony, and fulfill the admonition of the Apostle Peter: "Be ready always to give an answer to every man that asketh you the reason for the hope that is within you." Go over your testimony and get rid of the rough spots. Eliminate the trite saying. Get zip and life into it, and then ask God to help you use it. **In three minutes you should be able to effectively tell what you were before meeting Christ, how you met Him and what He has meant in your life since He saved you.**

HANDLING OBJECTIONS

When you present the Gospel, the arch foe will have his workmen doing their best to block your presentation. Fears and doubts will arise in your own heart and your prospect will raise objections. Earlier we have discussed how we handle our fears. In this chapter we will discuss what we do when an objection is raised. Our natural tendency is to meet an objection head-on and beat it down. This must be overcome for the sake of your prospect's eternal welfare. Negatively we say: **never argue.**

Often it has been said that the only way to win an argument is to avoid it, and the best way to avoid it is to preclude it. That is, anticipate it and lead your prospect to agree with the Scriptures before he can raise the objection. Any skillful debater can easily win a point in an argument, but by doing so you can arouse hostilities in the prospect that will cause you to lose your "fish."

A. How to Avoid Arguments

On the positive side you may meet every objection with: I'm glad you said that! You ought to be glad that your prospect has enough freedom to express his inner feelings to you. As you deal with his objections, you clear away the props which have deluded him into a presumptuous sense of security. You are glad when he shows he is listening and assimilating what you are presenting. Every

Avoid argument

Agree with adversary

89

objection can be met with, "I'm glad you said that!"

Of course, you must deal in some manner with the substance of the objection. If he raises a question which you will answer later in your presentation you may say, "I'm glad you asked that. It's encouraging to see your interest and I'm coming to that in just a minute. I think you will see it more clearly in the light of our present discussion on . . . " (whatever it is you are dealing with at the moment).

Outline: servant, not master

However, you need not be a slave to the Outline. You may show wisdom if you take up the matter "out of place." Often what is out of place in the printed presentation can be "in place" in the living situation.

Most often, however, your prospect will introduce matters on which you have not planned to talk. Suppose you are in the middle of the story of John Wesley's conversion and your prospect says, "I don't see why there have to be so many divisions in the church. Wesley started the Methodist Church which broke off from the Anglicans. And you're not a Methodist. Why can't you all get together?"

Don't panic

First, don't panic! Obviously this matter is extraneous; neither a discussion of church history and denominational origins, nor a discourse on the modern ecumenical movement would be of any value at this point. It is also obvious that you have lost your prospect's interest. Now you need to do two things. First, you need to get back on the track, and then you need to recapitulate so that your prospect may pick up your train of thought which he had lost. One approach might be:

Avoidance

"I'm glad you asked that for I can see it is something that would hinder your understanding of just what saving faith really is. I don't want to

90

mislead you as to what the key is that opens heaven's door. Now we've seen that neither intellectual assent nor temporal faith will open that door. You must trust the living Lord to do something for you. Just as Wesley had a certain kind of faith, he recognized that it was not saving faith. He wrote in his journal . . .''

In this manner you turn the conversation away from the extraneous matter and refresh his memory of what you were talking about before his mind wandered from your point.

Handle quickly

Another approach would be to deal quickly with the matter and return the conversation to the presentation at the point where you left it. ''I suppose just because we're human we will always have differences of opinion. It's interesting, though, that I can quote the founders of other denominations in presenting the Gospel to you. The mainstream of the Christian Church has been united for 2,000 years on the matters we've been discussing, such as man's sinfulness, God's holiness, and Christ's deity. The divisions have arisen on other matters, but we don't want them to cause you to go to heaven's door without the right key to open it, do we? For years Wesley thought he had the key to heaven. But it wasn't until after he worshiped in Aldersgate Street Chapel that he could write . . . ''

B. Answers to Common Objections

The heathen

Another extraneous matter that is commonly introduced is the heathen. If your prospect becomes uncomfortable as you talk about ''the heathen'' in his living room, he will likely try to start you talking about the heathen in India or New Guinea. Needless to say, such a tactic should never divert the evangelist from his objective. The woman at the well tried to change the subject when Jesus got close to her personal needs. He brought her back quickly by saying in effect, ''What we are doing here now is of much greater urgency than settling

91

a theological debate." This is "Pandora's Box." We dare not open it or we will never be able to share the Gospel.

In handling this matter you need to focus your concern on the indivdual you are witnessing to. "Bob," you might say, "that's a good question and I'm certain you have some interesting thoughts on it. However, my real concern right now is not some pagan who has never heard of Christ. Tonight I want you to know for certain that you have eternal life. The Bible says you can know that you have eternal life, and you have told me that you aren't sure what would happen if you died tonight. Let's confine our discussion to what God has said about you and your eternal welfare. Perhaps on another evening we can see all He has said about those who never hear the Gospel."

C. Precluding Objections

What are some of the common objections that arise? What are some ways in which we handle them?

The most common objection

Quite often we will get to the point of explaining what saving faith truly is and the prospect will say something like, "That's what I've always believed." Or, "That's what I said I was trusting in when you asked me." Obviously, you can't grab him by the lapels and cry, "Liar!" This comes up so often that we must take special care to get an answer to the question: "Suppose that you were to die tonight and stand before God and He were to say to you, 'Why should I let you into My heaven?' what would you say?" Not only must we get an answer, we must also understand the answer and get our propsect to agree that we understand what he is saying. There is no harm, after getting the answer to the question, in saying, "Now let me see if I understand you. You're saying . . . " Then rephrase what he has just said. He will either acknowledge or deny that your understanding is correct.

If you have sufficiently clarified the answer to "the question," your prospect is unlikely to reverse himself at the end and say, "Oh, I've always trusted in Christ for salvation!" Should he say this, one way to handle the situation is:

"Oh, I'm glad you said that. Apparently I misunderstood you when you said that you would tell God that He should let you into heaven because you keep the Commandments and live according to the Golden Rule."

Stress the difference

You may have to pursue the matter so that he becomes aware that he said he was trusting his good works and this is not compatible with trusting only in Christ. By God's grace he must arrive at the point of trusting Christ ALONE. As the hymn puts it: "Nothing in my hands I bring,/Simply to Thy cross I cling."

Another frequent objection is raised at the point of God's holiness and justice. "God isn't like that! He would never punish anyone." We need to realize that the biblical teaching of the just God "who will by no means clear the guilty" is unpopular even in many so-called Christian circles today. To deal effectively with this or any other open denial of biblical truth, you must appeal to authority. No help comes from saying, "I think you're wrong!" The matters under discussion are beyond what you think or what your prospect thinks. Assuming that he is a rational being of sound intelligence, what he thinks could be as valid as what you think. An external authority must be called upon to settle the matter.

Rationalism

You could proceed by saying, "How can we come to know about God? Well, there are two ways. One has come out several times in what you said. By thinking about God we can come to some conclusions about Him. We can say, 'I think God is all love and will send no one to hell.' Or, 'I think God is a demon and will send everyone to hell.'" Someone else may sit and think about God and conclude, 'I believe God is the sum total of human experience.' All this would be reasoning with no data in an effort to learn about God. This is the approach to knowledge which is known as rationalism.

"We could in a similar way reason about the color of eyes that any people of Mars may have. You think they're all red eyed. I might conclude they have polka-dot eyes. Your opinion is as good as mine because we have no data on which to base our conclusions. However, if somebody goes to Mars and returns and tells us that they have red, white and blue-striped eyes, then we have good reason for placing our confidence in this person who has been there. His conclusion is based upon data.

Revelation

"This is the other way in which we can come to the knowledge of God. He has come from where He is to where we are, and He has condescended to give us knowledge of Himself, His purposes and His will for us. This method is known as 'revelation.' For reasons I'll not go into now, the Christian Church has held that God did reveal Himself through the Scriptures and preeminently in His Son. So now the question is not what either of us thinks; rather, the question is, 'What has God said in the Bible and through His Son Jesus Christ?' "

"I don't believe the Bible"

Often as you begin presenting the Gospel, your prospect will say, "I don't believe the Bible. You'll have to convince me some other way than referring to the Scriptures." Many evangelists, ministers, as well as laymen, are devastated by this objection, and their attempt at presenting the Gospel fizzles. This need not be the case. Such an objection can be the springboard into the Gospel itself. The Apostle Paul, as he preached in the Greek cities, appealed to the Scriptures even though the people listening to him did not believe in the Scriptures. He did not try to convince his audience of the veracity and the authority of the

Scriptures. Rather, he proclaimed them, and the Holy Spirit worked and used the proclamation to save some who then believed the Bible to be true. **In witnessing, our primary function is proclamation, not defense.**

This is actually a rather easy objection to deal with. When it comes at the beginning of a presentation of the Gospel I would suggest that a person not use the approach of a boxer who would meet the blow head-on and try to overwhelm his opponent with counter punches, but rather that he use the technique of the judo expert wherein the force of his opponent's blow is used to throw him.

Use judo technique

The individual who uses this objection is usually a person who has had at least some college education and exposure to some course on the Bible, Biblical criticism or something of this sort. And there is usually an accompanying intellectual pride which says something like this: "I used to believe those fairy tales when I was in kindergarten but now I am an educated man and am far above believing such things." It is this intellectual pride which can be used to turn this objection into an opportunity for presenting the Gospel, somewhat as in the following illustration:

"You don't believe the Bible, Mr. Jones? That's very interesting and it certainly is your privilege not to believe it, and I would fight for that right on your part. However, if the Bible is true then obviously you must accept the consequences. But I would like to ask you a question. The main message of the Bible, which has been unquestionably the most important literary work in human history, is how a person may have eternal life. So what I would like to know is, 'Do you understand what the Bible teaches about this matter?' " He may reply that he does not believe in eternal life, to which you may respond, "I'm not asking you what you believe but I am asking you what you understand. It would be a rather unintellectual approach

"Do you understand the Bible message?"

to reject the world's most important book without understanding even its main message, would it not? Therefore, all I'm asking is, 'Do you understand the main message of the Bible which is how a person may have eternal life? What is your understanding about what the Bible teaches on this subject?' " In about 98 percent of the cases he will respond by saying that it is by keeping the Ten Commandments or following the Golden Rule or imitating the example of Christ, etc. You may then respond, "That is just what I was afraid of, Mr. Jones. You have rejected the Bible without even understanding its main message, for your answer is not only incorrect but it is diametrically opposite to what the Bible teaches. Now, don't you think that the more intellectual approach would be to let me share with you what the Scriptures teach on this matter and then you can make an intelligent decision whether to reject or accept it?"

Now the tables have been completely turned. Instead of being so superior to the Scriptures and above even listening to them, he now finds himself ignorant of even their basic message and must decide whether to listen to the message of the Scripture or be found to be not only ignorant but also an obscurantist who desires to remain in his ignorance. This is the last thing in the world that his intellectual pride will allow him to be; therefore, he will almost invariably give you permission to tell him the Gospel. At this point you pray mightily that the Holy Spirit will take the Gospel which is the power of God unto salvation and will use it to quicken him from the deadness of his sin.

Apologetic method

If this objection is raised toward the end of the presentation, then your answer will have to be quite different. We have found that the apologetic method of presenting the classical evidences of Christianity can be helpful at this point. For instance, you may read from the tract, "A Study in Prophecy," and then ask, "What have I just described?"

96

"The death of Christ," would be the obvious reply.

If you reveal that everything you read was from the Old Testament and was written hundreds of years before Christ was born, your prospect may be sobered to the point that you can deal with him about eternal life.

If a person does not believe in God's justice and hell, you may proceed to show that the prophets Isaiah (57:21) and Ezekiel (33:11), the apostles Peter (II Peter 2:4, 6, 9) and Paul (Romans 2:4, 5), and the Lord Jesus Himself (Mark 16:16; Luke 13:3; John 3:18, 36) taught that God will assuredly punish sin.

In dealing with the denial of the reality of hell, sometimes we find it helpful to say, "You know, it is a fact of psychology that we deny most passionately those things we fear most desperately. I wonder if the reason you don't believe in hell is that deep in your soul you fear that if there is such a place you may go there?" Often the reply is, "I guess you're right!"

"Hell isn't real"

You must go on then and assure our prospect, "I don't want you to believe in hell so that you can live your life in mortal terror of going there. You can know that you're not going to hell. That's what the Gospel is all about. I believe in hell but I know that I'm not going there because of God's promise. This is much better than saying, 'I know I'm not going to hell because I don't think there is such a place.' "

Occasionally you will meet a universalist who will object, "Everyone will be saved." This is the same objection we have been dealing with, only with a little different dress. Some Scripture that is useful in putting the lie to universalism is, "Then shall He say also unto them on the left hand, Depart from Me, ye cursed, into everlasting fire, prepared for the devil and his angels . . . these shall go away into everlasting punishment: but the

Universalism

righteous into life eternal.'' (Matthew 25:41, 46)

"The hour is coming, in the which all that are in the grave shall hear His voice, and shall come forth: they that have done good, unto the resurrection of life; and they that have done evil, unto the resurrection of damnation.'' (John 5:28, 29)

Stress the urgency

Often one will hear the Gospel and agree to its truthfulness but will not want to receive Christ at the moment. Of course, such an attitude is presumptive. The prospect assumes that he will have another opportunity to respond to God's gracious invitation. Probably he will; possibly he will not. The evangelist has a responsibility to press the urgency of the matter and persuade the prospect. Jesus warned of the fool who said, ''Soul, thou hast much goods laid up for many years; take thine ease, eat, drink, and be merry,'' only to hear the frightful words, ''Thou fool, this night thy soul shall be required of thee.'' Paul echoed the same thought: ''In the day of salvation have I succoured thee: behold, now is the accepted time; behold, now is the day of salvation.'' (II Corinthians 6:2)

Regardless of the form of the objection, recognize it as a device of Satan to prevent your proclaiming the Gospel. Recognize, further, that you are not calling on your prospect in order to defeat him in a debate. **By precluding objections and by dealing with those that arise in a matter-of-fact manner, you can succeed in presenting your prospect with enough information to make a decision.**

ILLUSTRATIONS

Following are a number of illustrations that we have found effective in illuminating the Gospel. The illustrations available for this purpose are limitless. Perhaps you will have good experience with some other illustrations. Since all of life is an illustration of spiritual truth, every sermon, book, or even the commonplace occurrences of everyday life provide abundant illustrations of spiritual truth. It should be noted that most illustrations are designed to point out one significant truth.

Imagine an orchestra playing in concert and suddenly one instrument is out of tune. The conductor would not eliminate the entire orchestra; however, he would have to cast out the bad instrument. Spiritually, we are out of tune with God. He is righteous; we are unrighteous. He is perfect; we are imperfect. God is sinless; we are sinful. Just as it was necessary to cast out the discordant instrument for the orchestra to remain an orchestra, it was necessary for the One in perfect harmony with Himself to cast man out. God cannot exist with sin. He can have nothing to do with that which is other than He is, and He is absolutely perfect, holy, and righteous.

God's holiness

You can liken our relationship to God as that of a mother who has carried her baby almost full term and then has a miscarriage. The mother has grown to love the child; she anticipates the fellow-

God's holiness

ship and presence of the child. However, the child has something in his biological makeup that actually acts in opposition to the mother's own biological makeup. This is the way it is spiritually. Man is actually a creature of God. However, man worked against God and introduced discord. Now God must cast away His creature. He still loves man, but if man remained in union with God it would destroy the perfection of God, and God would no longer be God.

Man's inability

Let the sofa and the coffee table represent the two sides of an incredibly deep canyon. Say the width is 100 feet. Now we can imagine every man, woman and child that has ever lived or ever will be born on earth is lined up on one side. They have to get to the other side, let's say, to save their lives from an impending danger. They will be lost if they don't make it. They have to jump. Now do you have any idea what the broad jump record is? Between 28 and 30 feet! How many people from the whole human race can jump the 100-foot-wide canyon? None! That's exactly right! No one would make it although some would do better than others. Some would jump way out— 20 feet or more. Some would only make it a few feet. Some cripples would just stumble over the edge. But none would make it! All would fall short of the mark. All would fall to their death.

This is the way it is spiritually. There is a gap between man and the Kingdom of God. We try as hard as we can to jump the gap. We go to church, keep the Commandments, don't intentionally hurt anyone, and jump out here as far as possible. That's the way I was in my own life— jumping hard! I had comfort from the fact that I was jumping farther than most. I figured God would accept those who jump the farthest. I knew no one is perfect so I figured He would accept those who did the best. I thought that God would lower His standard. But this would mean that God grades on the curve. He does not! I learned this

100

was wrong. He has only one standard: perfection. Jesus said, "Be ye perfect even as your Father in Heaven is perfect." I am not perfect. Suddenly I recognized that those people I looked down on who were not doing as well as I in being good were no worse off than I. I knew we were all going to the same death. Regardless of how good we are, none is good enough to get across the canyon. We are all doomed to the same eternal death. We will all go to hell if we have to make ourselves good enough for heaven. There must be another way across, or there is no way at all.

Man's inability

The reason we cannot keep God's Commandments is that we do not have the nature to act according to His will. We have no inner ability to keep them. Imagine that you have a lemon tree in your yard. All it can produce is sour lemons. Now if you want to grow oranges, you may decide to pull off all the lemons from your tree and then stick sweet, juicy oranges in their place. In a few minutes your tree could be covered with the sweetest oranges in town. Everyone looks and sees your "orange" tree—but in reality all you have is a lemon tree with dead oranges on it. You haven't changed the nature of the tree.

Our human nature is sour. Often we don't like it and we resolve to do better. We try to throw away the fruits of our sour nature. We get rid of the bottle, clean up our language and try to better family and business relationships. All we are really doing is picking off lemons and sticking on oranges. We get rid of bad habits and acquire good ones. However, this does not change the source of the stream of life. Our nature is untouched by our resolutions and reformations. We are as powerless to make our hearts good as we are to make a lemon tree into an orange tree. We need a new nature. The Bible says, "If any man be in Christ he is a new creation."

Man's inability

If the Central Intelligence Agency wanted you to be an agent behind the bamboo curtain in China, you would be trained to talk, act, look and think Chinese. You would go to school and learn the Chinese language so that you could speak it fluently without a trace of accent. After studying the mores of China and watching films of Chinese physical characteristics, you could duplicate their mannerisms. Perhaps you would undergo plastic surgery and have your face changed so that you would look Chinese. Then you could enter Communist China and be welcomed as one of them. You then would do everything in the Chinese manner. No difference would be noticeable. As far as anyone in China is concerned you are Chinese. Now let me ask you——would you be Chinese? No, not if you did not have Chinese parents. Nothing you can do will change your race.

Actually, it's the same way spiritually. You may talk and dress like a Christian. You may join Christian organizations and sing Christian songs, and in all ways act like a Christian. However, none of these things makes you a Christian. You were born a sinful man and you have the nature of a sinful race. Nothing you can do outwardly can change this fact. Just as you would have to have been born of Chinese parents to be Chinese, so you need a new birth spiritually to be a Christian. It's impossible for you to become a Chinese. However, with God all things are possible and you can be born anew spiritually and be a child of God. Those who have been born again put their trust for eternal life in Jesus Christ alone.

Christ's work

You can take the human predicament and make an equation out of it. Man's sinfulness plus God's justice can equal only one thing: eternal hell for man. That is what we deserve. However, there is another factor in the equation. If we add to man's sinfulness and God's justice the factor of God's love, again only one answer is possible: the Cross of Christ. Because God loved His people with an

102

everlasting love, it was necessary that Christ provide redemption through the blood of His Cross.

It is said that none ever could claim he was dealt with unjustly by the Areopagites in Athens. Their sentence always proved to be upright. How much more is this true of the righteous judgment of God who must be justified and all mouths stopped.

When Thomas Hooker lay dying, a friend said, "Brother, you are going to receive the reward of your labors." He humbly replied, "Brother, I am going to receive mercy." We need nothing but mercy, but mercy we must have or we are lost. Justice would give us what we deserve—hell. God in His infinite mercy and grace gives heaven.

A huge crowd of people were watching the famous tightrope walker, Blondin, cross Niagara Falls one day in 1860. Blondin crossed the rope numerous times—a 1,000-foot trip, 160 feet above the raging water. The story is told that he spoke to the crowd, asking if they believed he could take one of them across. Of course, they all gave their assent. Then he approached a man and asked him to get on his back and go with him. The man who was invited refused to go. It is like that with Jesus Christ. Mental assent, or even verbal assent is not enough. There must be trust—not strength—but trust in Christ alone.

Have you ever considered what makes faith valuable? Some seem to think that faith has an intrinsic value and they say, "Have faith!" I submit that faith must be in a valuable object if the faith itself is to be valuable. Faith in the wrong object is not valuable—it is disastrous. You may have all the faith you can muster in the brakes of your car; however, if the fluid line is broken your brakes will not stop the car and neither will your faith. If you awaken in the night with a headache and stumble

God's justice

God's mercy

Faith

1.Margaret Erb, Basic Christianity (Chicago: Inter-Varsity Press, 1952), p. 53.

into the dark bathroom, and in faith take a tablet which you think to be aspirin but mistakenly take a roach tablet, they may inscribe on your tombstone, "He died in faith," but your faith was in an object not worthy of your confidence. Many pregnant women took the mysterious drug thalidomide in the faith that it would make their pregnancy easier. Their faith did not prevent their bearing deformed children. Faith, to have any value, must be in a valuable object. When it comes to your eternal welfare only Jesus Christ is worthy of your confidence and trust. To have faith in anyone else or in anything is disastrous.

Good works

Good works cannot add to the gift of salvation. Suppose your best friend (or wife, husband, mother, etc.) were to surprise you with a beautiful gift, and let's suppose your response would be that of immediately digging into your purse or wallet for a couple of bills to help pay the expense. What an insult it would be! Suppose the gift was an expensive coat, and you offered back five dollars. This would result in wounding the giver. Well, what about offering one dollar—or say, twenty-five cents, or a nickel, or even a penny! No, the smaller the gift, the greater the insult. You must accept gifts freely. If you pay even a penny, it is not a gift. It is that way with salvation. Even a small attempt to pay for our salvation forfeits our receiving it. We will never be able to say one day in Heaven, "Look what Christ and I did!" It will be all Him—none of me. As God says in His word, "For by grace are ye saved through faith, and that not of yourself; it is the gift of God, not of works, lest any man should boast."

Good works

A famed cabinet maker is very fond of you. He wants to surprise you with the greatest gift you'll ever receive. Unknown to you, he gathers all the money he has. He takes all his life's savings, and though he has to deny his own son the privileges that others have, he sells all that he has, cashes in stocks and bonds, and hunts the world over to

find the best wood that money can buy. The priceless unfinished wood is brought into his shop. Day
and night he works to produce the most perfect,
the most beautiful table the world has ever known.
He goes without food, without sleep, and his
health is neglected. Finally, the cutting, the sawing,
the glueing, the fitting, and the sanding are all
done. He finishes this masterpiece by hours and
hours of hand polishing. Finally, the last stroke is
made with the cloth. The next day he comes to
your door with his men holding the table draped in
cloth. You welcome him in and he unveils the
priceless gift. What will be your response? Let's
say you run and grab a piece of sandpaper and
make a dive towards the table. This expert crafts-
man stops you short and exclaims, "It's finished!"
It is like this with salvation. God paid a priceless
sum in giving Jesus on the cross for us, who Himself cried out, "It is finished!" We can add nothing
—not one thing! We have only to receive—undeserving as we are. To change anything about that
gift of God is to refuse it. Where then is good
works? It is in the honoring of the giver. Just as
that table will be placed in the open for all to see,
and just as all who see it will be told all about the
glory and mercy of the man who made it, so we
will by the nature of our acceptance lift up God
in our lives and proclaim what He has done for us.
And this will be evidenced in all that we do and say.

DO'S AND DON'TS

After several years of "hitting our heads against stone walls" and finding that in many cases the same stone walls bruise our heads in the same way, we have searched for ways of avoiding the collision. Following is a list of some practical do's and don'ts that contribute to the success of our lay evangelism program.

Don't carry a large Bible on your visit! A New Testament **in your pocket or purse** will furnish all the Scripture you will need. A large Bible in your lap can have the same effect as a .45 revolver. Your prospect will wonder, "What's he going to do with that?" Never show your "weapon" until you are ready to use it. At the right time you can "draw and shoot him alive!"

Don't give the reference when you quote Scripture. You need to know the reference but giving the location of each verse that you use can interrupt your prospect's train of thought.

Do **quote just the relevant portion of the verse.** For example, we use I John 5:13 when we affirm that the Bible was written that men might know they have eternal life. We quote only: "These things are written that ye . . . may know that ye have eternal life." The rest of the verse would introduce matters not germane to the discussion at that point. People do not get all the meaning in a long verse. They can be easily lost. Concentrate on the portion of the verse that bears on the discussion at the moment.

Do anticipate objections and preclude them, if possible. When an objection arises deal with it in a manner that indicates that you are not threatened by it. **Handle objections in a straightforward, matter-of-fact manner and return to the main course of the discussion.**

Do **stress the positive benefits of the Gospel.** Some indicate by their manner of presentation that coming to Christ is one of the greatest disasters of life. Certainly this is not the case.

Don't use leading questions. If you know just a little psychology you can get your prospect to say yes to anything. However, you cannot manipulate a person into the Kingdom of God.

Don't use misleading questions. For example, "Tell me, Mr. Jones, what do you think you have to do to earn your way to heaven?" Such a question misleads your prospect. He may be trusting in Christ but you come with a voice of authority implying that he can do something to save himself. You have misled him. He may give you information that he does not truly believe, and the rest of your conversation would be in vain.

Do **start where the person is.** Do not assume that mid-twentieth century Americans know very much about the contents of the Bible.

Do **dangle your bait in front of the prospect.** Do not shove the hook down his throat.

Do **ask permission to ask questions.** It is wise also, occasionally, to ask your prospect's permission to continue dicussing the matters at hand, particularly if you sense some reticence on his part to continue. His simple "Yes" to "Would you like me to share with you what I learned about how to get to heaven?" will preclude his seething with rage as you proceed.

Do **ask your prospect's opinion.** He will feel more kindly to you if you indicate that you are an intelligent man who values his opinion.

Do **listen to your prospect talk** so that you can intelligently refer to statements he has made as you make your presentation.

Do **be conservative in your estimation of what happens on your visit.** You may see a profession of faith. Only time will tell if your prospect was born again, accepted the Lord and was converted.

Don't feel you have to secure a profession regardless of what you might have to do to get it. **High-pressure tactics are to be abhorred.**

Do **be overly modest as you talk about your church.** Do not convey the idea that yours is the only church that presents the Gospel.

Do **avoid critical comments about other congregations,** ministers, and denominations. It is true that many are unfaithful to the Lord. But you will lose your prospect's confidence if he feels you try to build your flock by tearing down others.

Do **smile, especially as you ask the two Questions.** If you are too intense, your prospect may feel he is being pinned down, and resent it.

Do **make your exit sweet**—even if the Gospel is rejected. Remember: it is the Gospel—not you—that has been rejected. The harvest is not until the end of the world—the prospect may yet be drawn to Christ.

Do **watch your grooming and manner of dress.** Sloppy shoes and unpressed suits do not speak well of the King you represent. Skirts that are too short can be distracting. Neatness is most important. A good rule: Dress in a way that will not draw attention away from your message.

Do **ask a friend if you have bad breath,** and encourage an honest answer. If you have it, do something to get rid of it or your prospect will be thinking of ways to get rid of you!

Don't sit in the car and pray before you go to the prospect's door. **Pray before you get to your prospect's residence.**

YOUTH EVANGELISM

A. Why a Gospel Presentation for Young People?

There are **two theological poles** to consider in **evangelism.** They are the objective and subjective elements (or the judicial and the regenerative aspects) of the Gospel. Both elements need to be included in our presentations. It is not a matter of either/or; it is a matter of both/and if we want to be biblical. However, the type of person with whom we are dealing will determine where emphasis should be placed. For instance, an adult will need to know "Why?" "What's the basis?" "I want the facts!" Hence with an adult we are heavy on the objective facts of the Gospel, the judicial aspect. For the most part, however, a young person (particularly a teen-ager) will want to know: "Does it work?" "Will it help me in my frustrating world?" Hence we need to lean heavily on the subjective elements, the **regenerative (new man) aspect.** Now, obviously, both need to be included always.

Therefore, the adult presentation of the Gospel is of the basic theme: "Eternal life—heaven." The basic theme in the youth presentation is "Fellowship with our Creator; friendship with Jesus Christ." Often with a young person one may find that **just the subjective** is needed—particularly if he is "ripe fruit." He has sensed conviction of sin; he is looking desperately for a Saviour, and just a short introduction of our Saviour's desire to enter his life as Lord and Master is sufficient. However, more often than not we talk with young people who may have just been awakened, and they need to know the objective facts of sin, separation, and substitution on which to base their experiences.

Following is, therefore, a presentation of the Gospel that **combines the subjec-tive-regenerative and objective-judicial elements** in a way that has proved to be, at least in measure, interesting and thought provoking to the young person and particularly the teen-ager. Such a presentation is needed not only for the young person who hears, but for the young person giving the witness.

B. Programs of Youth Evangelism

1. Junior High Programs

a. This program covers an eight-week period. Students are notified and asked to volunteer for an evangelism program. A big "kickoff meeting" is held and the young people are informed of the requirements to become a member. Select a name for the project. We called it "Operation Experiment", or "OX".

    a. Have quiet time each day;

    b. Memorize one verse each week;

    c. Attend OX each week;

    d. Attend at least one church service each week;

    e. Talk to one person each week about Christ (not necessarily whole presentation of the Gospel);

    f. Give testimony at a youth fellowship, social or church meeting;

    g. Learn to present the Gospel.

After a time of sentence prayers all young people turn in their printed pledge card—signed if they are entering the program, unsigned if they are not. The "signed" then meet each week one hour before the regular youth meeting, and follow a definite program of training. A check sheet of the requirements is held by each OX member. Three strikes—three misses on the requirements—and they are out of OX. This includes the youth sponsors. Simple written tests and practice presentations of the Gospel characterize the last four weeks. At the end of eight weeks a dinner is held for the remaining OX. A speaker is provided and testimonies are given as to what OX has meant to each member.

b. This program covers a three or four week period. We call it Operation "GO". The students meet at the church on Saturday mornings or afternoons for about an hour of instruction. After the instruction period there is a practical application of survey taken on the beach, shopping centers, or any place where large groups of people are found. Students need to be instructed to talk with their own peer group and their own sex. We encourage groups of three to five (co-ed) to operate together. The object in the survey is to get the Junior Highs talking to others on behalf of Jesus Christ. This excites Junior High kids enormously. The last Saturday is incorporated into a weekend program. Following is the schedule of our last Operation "GO" along with questions that may be used on a survey.

OPERATION GO!

JUNIOR HIGH

STARTS SAT. FEB. 28

ENDS ON WEEKEND OF MAR. 14

REGISTRATION FEE—$1.00

No Other Charge

SATURDAY FEB. 28

1:00 P.M.—YOUTH LOUNGE LUNCH
1:30 —DEMONSTRATION OF LEADING SOMEONE TO CHRIST
2:00 —GETTING STARTED
3:00 —CLOSE UP FOR THE DAY

SATURDAY MARCH 7

1:00 P.M.—LUNCH AT YOUTH LOUNGE
1:30 —GETTING CHRIST ACROSS TO OTHERS
2:30 —ORGANIZE TEAMS
3:00 —PRACTICAL APPLICATION
4:00 —SHARING

OPERATION "GO" CONFERENCE

FRIDAY MARCH 13

6:00 P.M.—PIZZA SUPPER
7:00 —OPERATION GO BRIEFING (PHASE #1)
8:00 —"GO!" #1
9:30 —REPORT AND SHARING
10:30 —HOME FOR BED

SATURDAY MARCH 14

8:30 A.M.—BREAKFAST AT JUNIOR HIGH HOME
9:00 —BRIEFING (PHASE #2)
10:00 —"GO!" #2
12:30 —LUNCH AT TEEN TOWER AND SHARING
2:00 —BRIEFING (PHASE #3)

SUNDAY MARCH 15

9:45 A.M.—WORSHIP SERVICE
11:00 —SUNDAY SCHOOL—SPECIAL REPORT
5:30 —REFRESHMENTS
5:45 —COLOR FILM
2:30 —"GO!" #3
4:00 —SHARING
6:00 —BANQUET AT TEEN TOWER
8:00 —OPERATION "GO" CLIMAX! SPECIAL VISITORS PROGRAM
10:00 —"GO" HOME

HAND IN WITH $1.00 BY FRI, FEB 26

NAME _____

ADDRESS _____

PHONE _____

SCHOOL _____

GRADE _____

WERE YOU IN OPERATION "GO" LAST YEAR?

YES _____   NO _____

STUDENT OPINION POLL

Date_____ Location_____ Male_____ Female_____ Approx. Age_____

1. What is your school?_____ Grade____

2. Do you live in this area? Yes ☐ No ☐ If yes, how long?_____

3. To what church or faith do you belong?_____

4. What do you know about (name of church sponsoring opinion poll)?

   _____

   Have you had any direct contact with_____church?

   (a) Sunday Worship _____
   If attended:
           Did you find anything hard to understand?_____
           Did you find anything helpful?_____

   (b) Teen Youth Program?_____

   (c) Can you suggest any way in which the_____church
       could help young people?_____

       _____

5. What is you ambition in life?_____

6. Do you believe there is a God? Yes ☐ No ☐ If yes, what is God like?

   _____

7. Do you ever pray? Yes ☐ No ☐ Do you read the Bible? Yes ☐ No ☐

8. In your opinion, what is sin? _____

9. Who was Jesus? _____
   Do you believe He is alive today? _____

10. In your opinion, what is "eternal life"? _____

11. Suppose you were to die tonight and stand before God and He were to say
    to you, "Why should I let you into my heaven?", what would you say?

    _____

12. Would you like for someone to share with you what the Bible teaches about
    eternal life and how you can know you have it? Now?_____Later?_____
    when?_____
              day   time

Name_____ Address_____Phone_____

The "GO" periods on Friday and Saturday are times when the Junior Highs saturate the area with invitations to the Saturday "Blast". Friday night, cars are used. On Saturday the church bus is used and the kids are let out with their teams along a given route. When the bus is empty, the first team is then retrieved and so on. It is a real thrill for each group to hear of the experiences of others as they board the bus.

2. Senior High Visitation

This is the most effective program that we have used with our Senior Highs. However, an appreciation first of the problems involved in Youth Visitation may help you in preparing a plan for your own church. The hindrances have been:

Having (even a few) teens who are interested in sharing Christ with others. It is not uncommon to have a high-school group of 15 or 20 with none desiring to share Christ or desiring to be really obedient to Christ in any area of their personal lives. To teach such as these has proven to be about as effective as holding a football clinic at a home for the aged. They'll sit and listen, but that's all.

When interest in such a program does emerge, we have found, first, that involvement in adult visitation is hard to schedule, and second, the rapport-getting methods are so vastly different that the teenager will miss perhaps the most beneficial part of training if he visits only with adults witnessing to adults. Also, the teenager will often be unimpressed by adult decisions for Christ. Teens usually think that most people will decide for Christ anyhow when they get middle-aged and older—out of the fun-loving "Pepsi generation" into the sad, overworked, needing-all-kinds-of-crutches-to-lean-on "Geritol crowd." Young people need to see their peers made alive through Christ. They need to see friends receive Christ—friends who they think would have no spiritual need—who would probably laugh at their witness, but who in fact are looking for Christ and will respond. Finally, the teenager will get little thrust to his witness if he simply helps out in somebody else's program. He needs his own program—something he can dig into and to which he can develop a loyalty as a member of a witnessing team.

Youth Visitation seems to be the answer to these problems. A book, "Evangelism for Teenagers," by Dr. Howard Ellis[1], touched off an all-out effort to begin a program. The plan presented by Dr. Ellis seemed practical and concrete,

---

[1] Dr. Howard W. Ellis, "Evangelism for Teenagers for a New Day," Abingdon Press

and we adapted it to our situation. We had been providentially guided through the prerequisite for such a program so that when it appeared we were ready for it. Following is the plan that was finally put together.

a. **Prerequisite**

Break through the sham testimonies of Christian teens by a conference and/or weekly programs designed to meet kids where they are in specific terms. Through Bill Gothard's Youth Workers Seminar in Chicago[2], we were helped to pick up these specifics in relating to teens the Christian life. Gothard pointed out that teens need to see their lives under God in these categories: (1) acceptance of self, (2) assurance of salvation, (3) goals in life, (4) harmony at home, (5) mature dating, (6) successful friendships.

We were finding that teens could take in everything we dished out, hear every great Christian speaker around, listen to hundreds of testimonies, be told of their responsibility to Christ, and yet remain inwardly bitter and rebellious toward God (not outward at all), have serious doubts about their salvation, never consider what God would have them do with their lives, be primary causes of continuous strife in their homes, follow loose dating practices, and keep pretty bad company as their real friends.

This would not be too unusual for some teens today, but when this same teen can give you his testimony of salvation and see no discrepancy in it, then something is very wrong. Jesus Christ is Lord of his spirit, but not Lord of his life. To make a teen go and do anything for Christ in this condition can drive him even further from Christ. To yell in the ear of such a person that he must witness may drive him to torment, but he cannot go out and tell lies about Jesus Christ—things about Christ that his parents and teachers say are true but he is almost sure they're not.

We must be quick to realize, however, that such a person described above, who outwardly follows along in a witnessing program, will soon come face to face with himself and either quit the program or go on with the painful examination which must follow in order that he may be an effective witness for Christ. There is no doubt that this has proven good therapy in some cases, but it is no way to begin a program.

The solution to this problem is to continuously hit three categories mentioned above. You will find if you do that you will be "scratching teens where they itch," to quote Paul Little in "How to Give Away Your Faith." These categories of life must be completely delved into with something on hand each time—

---

[2] Campus Teams Institute in Basic Youth Conflicts: Instructor, Bill Gothard. 1027 Arlington Ave., LaGrange, Illinois 60525

something that must **never** be left out: God's Word spoken to the area of life examined. The moment teens see that God is living life with them, and they are willing to be honest with themselves, the rest will begin to come.

After a weekend conference of this nature, with no speaker but the Bible and with thought-provoking questions, one teen girl witnessed the next week at school for the first time in months. Her method was a little wild, though. She tried to explain I Peter to a non-Christian friend, Another teen, who has been a Christian for several years, said, "I feel as though I've never read the Bible before." Now we're ready to teach sound methods as to how this exciting life in Christ can be effectively communicated from one teen to another.

b. Senior High Visitation Weekend Conference (Operation Key)

1. Preparation

Several weeks before "Operation Key," the senior highs were told that on the last weekend in January we were going to have a weekend conference at the church. They looked puzzled. We continued, "You will only sleep at home; every other hour and every meal will be at the church." They had never done this before. It did not sound too exciting. A couple of weeks later it was announced that we were going to have a speaker that weekend but he was not to be for us. He was to be speaking on Saturday night of the conference weekend only to those non-Christians whom we got to come and hear him. We then explained to the officers of the group what we were planning.

They began to be as excited as we were over the possibilities. As the weekend neared the officers began to talk to the other teens. One large factor in the success of the weekend was a 6 A.M. prayer breakfast that was attended by the officers in the home of the senior high sponsors. This meeting was held on Wednesday, Thursday and Friday on the week of the conference.

The name "Operation Key" was simply gotten from the similarity in sound to the visiting speaker's name. Then "Key" began to be easy to build on. Posters were made and conference folders were mailed. Slowly but surely we had 20 sign up (most of them reluctantly). The cost of the conference was a ridiculous $1—any higher cost would cause some young people to eat meals at home. We wanted them together all the time. The dollar was simply for a registration token of commitment to the weekend. Needless to say, our cost was a drain on the budget, but it paid off.

2. **Conference Schedule** (fit this to your own situation)

Friday evening
4:30 Operation Key Briefing
(Phase 1)
5:00 Speaker
6:00 Fellowship Supper
7:30 Operation Key In Action #1
9:30 Report and Sharing Time
10:00 Prayer Time
10:30 Home for Bed

Saturday morning
8:00 Breakfast in the Church
8:30 Operation Key Briefing
(Phase 2)
9:00 Speaker
10:00 Operation Key In Action #2
12:00 Lunch
Report and Sharing Time

Saturday afternoon
1:00 Recreation
1:30 Operation Key Briefing
(Phase 3)
1:45 Speaker
2:30 Operation Key In Action #3
4:30 Report and Sharing

Saturday evening
6:00 Fellowship Banquet
8:00 Operation Key Climax
Speaker (Visitors attending)
10:30 Operation Key Briefing
(Phase 4)
11:00 Home for Bed

Sunday morning
9:30 Sunday School
11:00 Worship Service

Sunday evening
6:30 Operation Key In Action #4
7:00 Evening Service
8:30 Fellowship Meeting and
Refreshments in the youth
lounge with speaker

The speaker times were informal talks on commitment by the guest speaker, except, of course, for the Saturday night meeting—the big meeting for non-Christians. This meeting was evangelistic.

The "In Action" times were visits made to teens in the area. Starting a month before, names and addresses of teens were collected from church members who knew of them as neighbors, friends, etc. These were all put on one type of card, organized into geographic groups, and sent out with teams to be visited. The number of teams was determined by the number of cars available and the number of licensed drivers. Four or five in a car worked out an alternating visit system. Teams should be co-ed groups.

Visits #1 and #2 were not evangelistic visits, but were designed to get the visitors' "feet wet." Professionally printed cards showing time and place of meeting and other attractive information were carried by all visitors. They knew their goal was to get these teens to the Saturday night meeting. Those who said they would come were offered a ride. The Saturday visit #3 followed the same pattern but was to be an attempted evangelistic visit.

The youth lounge is an old engine room of a former firehouse done over into a youth lounge. This "hang out" area is very advantageous with teens. However, for a weekend conference such as this any large room given over completely to youth for the weekend will serve well. There must be games, etc., for recreation sandwiched in the busy schedule.

3. **Results**

a. Those who showed for the conference came in a relatively sober mood, knowing that it was all theirs. This is something we couldn't do——go out and get their peers. They were teen responsibilities. **This cut out many who were not willing to pull the load;** this in itself was progress.

b. **The visitors found that other teens did not reject their invitations,** but were almost always pleasantly surprised that someone cared enough to make a visit. This scored a real victory.

c. **So many responded to the friendship visits** that **our kids** ditched the visitation cards and **started visiting their "real friends."** This was a real breakthrough.

d. **Our "group" became a group.** Some learned the last names of others in the group and began to recognize them as people instead of just other persons forced on them by circumstances. Going on a difficult mission together really brings people together in the Lord.

e. **They learned to appreciate what is involved in getting the Gospel message to others,** and it set them up for real personal evangelism instruction.

f. **They learned the power of the Holy Spirit.** One girl ran from her car after the Saturday P.M. evangelistic visit and with tears in her eyes said, "It worked! I made my own opening for Christ. I was bold and not passive. For the first time I carried the ball, and she listened and wants to accept Christ." On the same visit, two boys sat in the car and prayed. They said they felt a strange sensation that they were just as much a part of that visit as the girl who spoke for Christ as they felt through faith that God was answering their prayers.

g. **Six made decisions for Christ on Sunday night.** These were teenagers who were brought to our church by these visits. The fact that several received Christ was almost incidental to the thrill these teams experienced as they felt God could move in them personally and as a group.

h. **Speaking out for Christ has become a part of the life of several** in the senior high group. For the first time, they are beginning to ask us if they can share with the group what Christ means to them.

i. **Evangelism classes have been requested** by the senior highs. This request is being carried out on Wednesday nights and we trust will grow through its rough edges to become a vital part of our youth program. Here is the schedule.

Wednesday P.M.
4:30 Youth lounge open for informal recreation
5:45 Go get supper (hamburgers, pizzas, etc.)
6:00 Eat
6:15 Instruction period and prayer
7:00 Visit
8:45 Return and share
9:15 Home

c. Leadership

It must not be assumed that this program will automatically work. The lay adult youth advisers determine everything, humanly speaking, as far as success is concerned. To recruit and train youth workers in a church is by far the most difficult part of a youth program. Time and energy by the carloads is needed. Not many are willing to give it. Teens will never respond to those who are working with them under the sense of duty. The worker must like teenagers, and such workers are rare. Some churches put such a burden on the most experienced workers (which so often are great candidates for youth work) that there is no time left for anything else. **It takes time to get to know teens** and if the worker is not constantly with them he fails to be effective. Our Lord with His disciples is a good case in point, and it has been proven to be the same today, over and over again.

Another tough requirement for a youth worker is that his life must be examined before the Lord. He must be honest with teens, and to do that he must be honest with himself and God. Teenagers mirror our own lives more easily than any other group of people. You will never see a hypocrite work very long with young people in a direct person-to-person basis. Teenagers are exciting because they are so real, and though they cannot or will not see inconsistencies in themselves they will not tolerate such inconsistencies in others.

C. Presentation of the Gospel for Youth

Outline

I. Introduction
   A. Their secular life
   B. Their church life
   C. Questions:

1. If you were to die today and stand before God, and He said, "Why should I let you into my heaven?" what do you think you would say?

2. Have you gotten to that place in your life where you know that if you were to die today you would go to heaven?

D. Testimony

II. Gospel

  A. Man's problem

    1. Our separation — "For all have sinned and come short of the glory of God." Romans 3:23

    2. Our helplessness — "As it is written, there is none righteous, no, not one." Romans 3:10

    3. Our punishment — "Cursed is every one that continueth not in all things which are written in the book of the law to do them." Galatians 3:10b

  B. God's solution

    1. Christ was one with God — "I and My Father are one." John 10:30

    2. Christ was punished in our place — "All we like sheep have gone astray; we have turned every one to his own way; and the Lord hath laid on Him the iniquity of us all." Isaiah 53:6

    3. Christ is the only way to God — "Jesus saith unto him, I am the way, the truth, and the life: no man cometh unto the Father, but by Me." John 14:6

  C. Our part

    1. I must acknowledge my sin — "I came not to call the righteous, but sinners to repentance." Mark 2:17b

    2. I must trust Christ alone for my salvation — "For God so loved the world, that He gave His only begotten Son, that whosoever believeth in Him should not perish, but have everlasting life." John 3:16

    3. I must receive Him as Saviour and Master — "But as many as received Him, to them gave He power to become the sons of God, even to them that believe on His name." John 1:12

III. The Close

  A. Lead them through Revelation 3:20 — "Behold, I stand at the door, and knock: if any man hear My voice, and open the door, I will come in to him, and will sup with him, and he with Me." Revelation 3:20

  B. Lead them in prayer

  C. Lead them through I John 5:11-13 — "And this is the record, that God hath given to us eternal life, and this life is in His Son. He that hath the Son hath life; and he that hath not the Son of God hath not life. These things have I written unto you that believe on the name of the Son of God; that ye may know that ye have eternal life." I John 5:11-13

Presentation

(Jack, evangelist; Ted, non-Christian)

I. Introduction

Hi, Jack!

What do ya' say, Ted?

Not much. Sure was a rough day today.

Yeah, sure will be good when school gets out, won't it?

Yeah, I'll sure like that. Boy, I just knew I'd flunk that English paper I had to write today.

You flunked your test?

Yeah, I really blew it. I thought I'd done real well, too.

How come you flunked it?

Well, I don't know. The teacher didn't pick the right topic so I wrote on the telephone book.

The telephone book? That's not much of a story——in the telephone book.

Well, I admit it doesn't have much of a plot. But it's sure got plenty of characters. She didn't seem to like that . . . she's sort of an old bag anyway. She's Mrs. Baugh. Did you hear of her?

Yes, I've heard of Mrs. Baugh. She's a hard teacher.

Yeah, that's right. Not only is she real tough in English but she sorta talks about religion all the time, too.

Religion? Well, that's interesting.

It gets sorta corny sometimes, sittin' there listenin' to her in class. Talk about this . . . talk about that . . . I get a little tired of it.

Are you waiting on a ride or something, Ted?

Yeah, I'm sittin' here waiting.

A. Their religion and church life

You know, I've been thinking about some things. You talk about this religion stuff. Did you ever talk to Mrs. Baugh about religion?

No, not really. She just makes remarks about how everybody ought to go to church on Sunday. It's not very interesting.

Well, I used to feel like you, too, Ted. Do you go to church anywhere?

Oh, yeah, yeah . . . I go to church just about every Sunday with my family.

Really?

Yeah, I've been going to church ever since I've been about knee-high to a grasshopper.

Have you gone to Sunday school, too?

Yeah, I go to Sunday school. We've been going to church, ah, on State Road 7. It's called, ah, St. John's in the Fields, or something like that. I don't remember the name of it. It's a Presbyterian Church. My parents have been going there, and I've been going over there just about every Sunday.

B. Questions

Well, that's interesting. May I ask you a question, Ted?

Sure, go ahead.

I've been thinking a long time about asking you this question. And I don't know how you'd answer this. Maybe you never thought about something like this before. I thought about this not too long ago, and it really got me to thinking. You've been in church and all, and Sunday school. Let me ask you and see what you'd say. **If you were to die today and stand before God, and He said, "Why should I let you into My heaven?", what do you think you would say?**

That is a pretty good question. I guess I'd say that I've been going to church, or my parents have been making me go every Sunday, or about every Sunday. I guess this would be a help . . . a step in the right direction. I'm not too bad of a guy. I mean, on Halloween I go out and do a few things destructive. Just sort of prankish stuff. Soap up windows on stores downtown. I'm not really a bad guy. Every now and then I go out to the beach, and maybe do some things down there I shouldn't do. But I think pretty much in all . . . I don't really know. I mean, honestly . . .

If you stood before God, then, and He were to say, "Why should I let you into heaven?" you'd tell Him that you lived as good as you were able?

Yes, I've lived a pretty good life. I would do most anything for anybody. I'm honest, not a hypocrite. I've gone to church pretty much, and a . . . I've just been a pretty good guy. But, like everybody, I'm not perfect, or anything.

All right. Do you mind if I ask you another question, Ted?

No.

This is one that got me really thinking. I tried to avoid people who asked it of me. But I'll throw it out to you and see what you'd say. **Do you think you have gotten to that place in your life where you know that if you were to die today that you would go to heaven?**

Oh, yeah, I'd probably go to heaven.

You're sure you would?

Yes, I'd probably go to heaven.

You're definitely sure?

Well, I don't think anybody can be sure. How can someone be really sure they're going to go to heaven?

C. Testimony

The reason I asked you this is because I think you're exactly at the place where I was not too long ago. I thought that a person who knew he was going to heaven, knew that he was going to be with God forever, was sort of "kooky," you know. There's something about him that . . . I mean, he was pretty conceited.

Like Mrs. Baugh . . . a fanatic?

124

Does she know that she is going to heaven, Ted?

> Yeah, I heard her tell somebody that in the lunchroom once. It's crazy.

I used to think that a person like that was cocky and fanatical and everything. But listen, Ted, let me explain something to you. A person **can know** that they will be with God forever. Do you think your ride will be here in a minute?

> Oh, I've got a few minutes. The bus is usually late. Go ahead. How can anybody know they're going to heaven?

II. The Gospel

A. Man's problem

Let me explain it to you this way. First, we need to see that man has a problem, and here it is. The Bible says that we were made for God. All men everywhere were made for God. If I just let my right hand represent God and my left hand represent man, the Bible says that man was made for God and he lived with God like this (placing left fist in right hand). And this is not my opinion . . . this is what the Bible says. The Bible says that we were made for God.

1. Our separation

All right, here's what happened. The Bible says that man broke this relationship—that he and God were one together, but that they were separated from each other. They were separated because man got out of tune with God. He rebelled against God's perfect will and direction for his life. This would be like a parade going down the street or like the band at half-time at a football game. One man is out of step and his instrument is out of tune. Well, they might like the guy in the band, but as long as his instrument is out of tune, they're going to have to tell this fellow to leave, in order for the band to sound good. Now if God is going to remain God, and man is rebelling against God . . . wanting to go the other way . . . is out of step with God . . . out of tune with God, the only way for God and His Kingdom to remain perfect and in harmony is that man must leave the kingdom of God. Because man is out of step and out of tune with God, man was separated from God. So here's what happened. Man was separated from God and we're all born right here. (With the right hand high, the left fist is drop-

125

ped from the grasp of the right hand to a low position. The left hand now is "man after the fall." We're all born here.) You know, Ted, most people think that everybody is born here (drawing attention to the right hand still held up and now representing God and His Kingdom). The Bible says that everybody is born apart from God—down here. God does not hate man—He loves man. But if He is to remain holy, righteous, and perfect, then He cannot allow us to be in a relationship with Him because we are unholy, unrighteous and imperfect.

2. Our helplessness

The next thing we need to see about man's problem is this: man is separated from God, and he can't get back to God. As hard as he may try, man cannot get back to God. Man is helpless to work his way to God. Let's use these two big rocks here for an illustration. Now, I'll show you what I mean. Let's say this rock and this rock are 100 feet apart. We'll say that between them is a bottomless canyon and that the two rocks are the two sides of the canyon. Do you know what the world's record broad jump is? You run track, Ted?

Yeah, about 28 to 30 feet.

All right, about 28 to 30 feet. Now, it's 100 feet across this canyon, and we're going to take every human being that ever lived or will live and line them up shoulder to shoulder on this side of the canyon. Now if they all tried to jump across over to this other side, 100 feet away . . . if they were to try to jump that far, how many would make it?

Not anybody would make it. No one.

That's right. Some would jump farther than others. Some would just fall over the edge; some would get in the 20-foot range. No one would make it; all would come short. Do you realize, Ted, that we daily break the laws of God? You and I have broken every one of the Ten Commandments. You haven't killed anybody, but Christ says in Matthew in the Sermon on the Mount that if you hate someone in your heart, you've killed them. Christ said also if you look on a girl to lust after her you've committed adultery in your heart. And we've broken the other commandments—obeying parents, keeping the Sabbath, stealing or cheating—and a day doesn't go by that we haven't had some god before us instead of our Creator—gods like clothes, friends, and making the ball team.

Anything our life revolves around is our god. We've broken God's laws, you see. If not outwardly, we've broken them inwardly.

3. Our punishment

If a person remains like this, separated from God, and dies like this, He will be apart from God forever. And he will never be able to be in the presence of God—the One for whom he was made and One whose love he needs. And so the problem man has, you see, is that he's separated from God, he can't get back to God on his own strength, and we're told that if he doesn't come back to God he will live apart from God forever. The Bible says this is hell. You see, God is not only loving and forgiving but He is just. Let me cite an example. A judge downtown will tell us if we commit a crime that we have to pay, say $25, for some law we've broken. Ted, let's say you were standing before a judge that was going to fine you $25 for a crime you had committed. If the judge knew you, would he still fine you?

Yeah.

Let's say he knew your family real well and loved all of you. Would he still fine you?

Yeah, I think he would.

Okay, let's say he's a good man, honest, and has a forgiving heart. Would he still fine you?

Yes. I see what you mean.

You see, he is loving and forgiving, but he would be crooked if he did not fine you. You broke the law and you must be punished, even by a loving judge. You have to pay $25. It is the same way with God. He is loving. He loves us and He wants us to be with Him, And life doesn't make sense without Him. But He can't allow us to be with Him, because we have to pay for our sins. This means that we are to be punished—separated from Him—forever. This is the worst thing that can happen to anyone—this is hell. Now the problem is, how can a loving God allow us to come to be with Him and at the same time be a just God and send us to hell?

B. God's solution

Well, God has solved this problem. God did a fantastic thing—He came into the world in person.

1. Christ—one with God

This person came right from God's presence and He said that He and the Father were one. In the Gospel of John He says, "I and the Father are one." His name was Jesus Christ and He was one with God. And what Jesus Christ did, Ted, was go to the cross and He died there. Now listen to this. He came right into the position we're in and He was separated from God eternally, because He was an eternal Being.

2. Christ punished in our place

And He went to hell for you and me on the cross. The Bible says that God "hath laid upon Him the iniquity of us all." If we let this little book represent that which contains all of your sins, then every one of your sins were laid upon Jesus Christ. (Swap the book from one hand to another, showing how Christ took all of our sins on Himself.) He died in your place. He substituted for you. He took all of your sins upon Him. Let me show you how clearly the Bible records this. The Thursday night before His death He prayed in the Garden of Gethsemane, saying, "Abba, Father . . ." Abba, if accurately translated, means "Daddy." Jesus was this closely related to His Father in heaven, but that next afternoon on the cross Jesus Christ said, "My God, My God, why hast Thou forsaken Me?" Jesus Christ was split from God on the cross. He went to hell in our place. He never said "God" before to His Father and He was never confused; this shows that something happened to Christ on the cross—after He was nailed there. The Bible says God sent Him into hell in our place so we wouldn't have to go. Christ let the Roman soldiers spit on Him, slap Him around, whip Him, mock Him, and nail Him on a cross. He let God punish Him in our place, because He loved us so much. On Thursday night, Jesus said, "Father if there's another way for people like Ted and Jack to come to you, then do it another way. Not my will, though, but your will be done." Ted, there was no other way.

3. Christ—only way to God

This means, Ted, that Jesus Christ is our only way to God. Jesus paid for your sins, and He is the only way to God. The Bible says that "there is no other name under heaven given among men whereby we must be saved." Christ said also, "I am the way, the truth, and the life. No one can come to the Father but by Me." He is the only way to God. He does not show us the way. He **is** the way.

C. Our part

Now you see that we've got a problem? And you see that God solved the problem? Jesus Christ died for our sins. And you see that there is no way but Christ back to God? The Bible says that Satan knows all we've talked about and he trembles, and he doesn't belong to God. Then what must we do to get back to God? Well, this is our part.

1. I must acknowledge that I am a sinner

The Bible says that we need, first of all, to acknowledge to God that we are helpless, that we are separated from God, and that we are helpless to get to Him. It means that we must admit we are lost. If I were to tell you, Ted, that you would be shot tomorrow if you didn't swim across Lake Okeechobee in the next 24 hours, do you think you would try to swim across the lake?

Yeah.

Are you sure you'd make it?

No.

It would be rough, wouldn't it?

It would be tough.

But you would swim for your life. All right. Suppose I told you that you had to dive in right here at the Atlantic Ocean and swim to England by tomorrow night, in the next 24 hours. Would you try to do it?

It would be impossible.

You wouldn't even try to do it, would you?

I don't think so. No.

Because, you see, you would **know** you could not make it. It's only when you think that maybe you might make it that you try. If you know you wouldn't make it at all, you would quit and look for another way. Now, if you think that maybe you can make it to God by the good life that you live and all the good things that you do in your life——that maybe you'd be good enough to be with God forever, then you will continue to try to live as good a life as you can in order to get there. But the Bible says you're lost. The Bible says "all have sinned and come short." Some have jumped farther than others, but all have come short. Some have lived better lives than others, but all have come short of the glory of God. Now that means this: if you were to find out that you could **not** get to God by all you did, you'd look for another way. That's why a person must acknowledge to God, must agree with God, that he can't get to Him on his own, that he is a sinner, that he is lost. The minute we do that we will have to start looking for another way. And Jesus said, "I am the way." Christ is the only way to God.

2. I must trust Christ alone for salvation

The Bible says that we need to put our trust in Jesus Christ alone for our salvation. You know, when I asked you that question a minute ago, do you know what your answer was, Ted? I said, "Ted, what reason do you have to go to heaven?" You know what you said? You said you lived a pretty good life, you had gone to church, you hadn't done anything real bad, you'd prayed, you'd read your Bible——you see, you're your own Saviour. The Bible says that **Jesus Christ**——not you——has to be your Saviour. You need to trust Him and not the good things you've done. Let's take that rock——that big rock by the bus stop. Ted, do you believe that rock is there?

Sure!

Do you believe the rock will hold you?

Of course!

Is it holding you right now?

No. because I'm not on it.

Right. You have to be on the rock for it to hold you.

Right.

Like you, Ted, I know the rock is right there. I believe it's a strong rock. I believe it will hold me. But is it holding me?

No, it's not.

Let's say that I've seen that rock every day for a year, that I've even put my books on it to lighten my load while I've waited for the bus, but I've never sat on it. You see, even then I've never been held by the rock because I've never trusted myself to it. But I have trusted myself to this bench I'm sitting on. This bench is holding me. Ted, it's easily possible that though you believe in Jesus Christ as God's only Son, and have gone to church to learn of all He did, and though you are convinced that He died for the sins of the world—you can know all that and yet never have trusted Him. I was that way. And that would mean you're still separated from God and lost. Just like knowing about the rock and letting it hold my books; I knew about Christ and I gave problems to Him to help lighten my load, but what was I depending on? I was depending upon my own good life—just like I'm depending on this bench right now to hold me! Why should I get to heaven, I used to think. Well, I had prayed, I read the Bible every now and then, I went to church, I was baptized and a member of the church. I was a good guy. I tried to keep the Commandments, I tried to help others, I-I-I-I-I-I. You see, I was my saviour. I knew all about Christ (pointing to the rock)—believed every word He said, but was trusting me—my good life (pointing to the bench). It was then that the truth of John 3:16 began to dawn on me. "For God so loved the world, that He gave His only begotten Son, that whosoever **believeth** in Him should not perish, but have everlasting life." That word "believe," Ted, means "trust," "to commit yourself to" Jesus Christ.

Just like moving from this bench to that rock, I must transfer myself completely into the hands of Jesus Christ. (Jack moves to the rock.) Now, Ted, the only thing holding me up is the rock —it's all that is between me and the ground. I am just as strong as the rock is. It is like this with Christ. I must trust Him with myself—not just my problems—but myself, so that He alone is between me and eternal damnation. And since my salvation is just as strong as He is, then that's as strong as I ever need.

131

I have eternal life because I'm committed to Christ. I've transferred my trust to Him.

3. I must receive Christ as Master and Lord

And then the last thing is this. I need to allow Jesus Christ to be the **Lord** as well as the Saviour of my life. Suppose that I've got a motorcycle at home. Do you have a motorcycle, Ted?

Sure!

All right, Ted, if your motorcycle is broken, and it's something that you couldn't fix, and you took it to a mechanic and said, "Mac, I want you to fix this motorcycle, but please don't touch the motor," do you think he would start work on it?

That's sort of ridiculous, isn't it?

Right! Mac would say to go to some other guy to get it fixed. He wouldn't fool with it. If you're going to try to get the motorcycle fixed, you have to let Mac have the whole motorcycle. Now it's like that with us and Christ. We can't come to Jesus Christ and say, "Lord Jesus, I want you to do this and that in my life. Here is a problem for you to take——here's a crisis in my life, but, Lord, please don't bother these other things in my life. I'm controlling them!" If you said this to Him, Ted, He would answer, "Ted, I've got to have your whole life. If you want me to wash you and to cleanse you and to make your life run the way I want it, I've got to have your whole life." This is what the Bible means by "believe." Jesus Christ said that you have to commit your whole life to Him, and He has to be not only your Saviour but your Master——the Lord and Master of your life. He loves us, and He knows our every need. But until we give ourselves to Him, He cannot be our Saviour and Friend.

That's sort of hard to do, isn't it?

III. The Close

That's a good question, Ted. How can we do this? What is it that we need to do right now? Ted, do you really believe that in your own heart you're a sinner?

Based on what you've said, yes!

Do you believe that you are separated from God?

Yes.

Do you believe that you can't get back to God on your own—that you're helpless to do that?

It would be pretty hard, eh? Impossible!

And you believe that Jesus Christ lived, and died for your sins, and without Him you would be lost forever?

Yes.

All right. Are you willing for Jesus Christ to really come into your life?

I'd like that very much.

Are you willing to give your life to Him forever? Do you want Jesus Christ to be your Lord and Master?

Yes.

A. Lead them through Revelation 3:20

Now the question is, what must you do right now? Let me get you to read a verse. There's a little New Testament I have here. (Jack reaches into his pocket.) Read this verse out loud so that you'll be sure to get every word of it. I've got a mark there by the verse.

"Behold, I stand at the door and knock. If any man hear My voice and open the door, I will come in to him and will sup with him and he with Me."

All right. In this verse, who's knocking at the door?

"Behold, I stand at the door and knock." I am.

Well, if you look back up in those verses, you'll see that it's someone else knocking. Let me help you at this point. If you were to read that whole chapter, you'd find out that it is Jesus Christ who's knocking at the door. He says he is knocking at the door of our life. He is knocking at the door of your life right now. And he says, Ted, that He wants to come into your heart and He wants to be your Saviour and your Friend. That verse says that He wants to sup with you and you with Him.

What does that mean?

That verse couldn't be written very well in our day because we eat at the Steak House and MacDonald's and all these places . . . we eat in three minutes and with strangers. But in those days, when you went to eat with somebody, it was often an all-day affair and with close friends. Jesus Christ said that He wants to have that kind of a close fellowship with us. He wants to be a real friend. He wants to come into your life and share life with you. In that verse, Ted, what do you have to do in order for Him to come in?

"If any man hear My voice, and open the door" . . . eh . . .

So what do you have to do?

First I have to hear Him and then open the door. This would be my willingness for Him to come into my heart.

All right, are you willing for Him to come into your heart?

Am I willing right now? . . . Yes, I am!

All right, what do you have to do right now, according to that verse? What is the only thing that you have to do?

Open the door?

Yes, just open the door.

How do you do that?

That's another good question. Suppose somebody came to your home one day and they knocked on the door, how would you let them in?

Just open it up.

All right. Now suppose you locked the door and asked them to come in?

They couldn't get in.

That's right. So it means unlocking the door, opening it up, and they will come in. And that's what Jesus Christ says in this verse, that if you will unlock the door of your life and open your heart to the Lord Jesus, He will come in.

B. Lead them in prayer

Now, Ted, Jesus Christ is with us right now. He's right here with us. And I think the thing to do is just to talk to Him—just like we would talk to each other. If it would be all right with you, why don't we pray and I'll just tell the Lord—He's right here—what we've been talking about. He already knows anyway. We'll just ask Him to come into your life. Right now. Would you be willing for that?

Yes, I sure would.

O.K., why don't we pray now?

O.K.

Lord Jesus, we thank You that You are here right now. You know Ted's heart and You know that he needs You and he wants You to come into his heart and his life, and I pray that You will help him to open the door of his heart . . . Ted, while we're praying, why don't you pray in your own words . . . it might sound kind of strange . . . you may not have prayed out loud before . . . but no matter how you say it, just talk to Jesus using His name. He's right here with us. Just tell Him that you want Him to come into your heart—into your life—to cleanse you of your sins. Just say that in your own words and address Him personally out loud. I'll wait.

(Silence) . . . Dear God . . . Jesus . . . I ask . . . help me. Jack, I don't know how to pray very well.

All right. I'll help you, Ted. Just pray after me because I think this is just what is on your heart.

Lord Jesus.
    Lord Jesus.
I know that I'm separated from God.
    I know that I'm separated from God.
I know I have sinned againt You.
    I know I have sinned against You.
I am helpless to come to God.
    I am helpless to come to God.
And I know You died for me.
    And I know You died for me.
Come into my life.
    Come into my life.

135

Cleanse me.
Cleanse me.
Wash me of my sins.
Wash me of my sins.
Do whatever You want to with me.
Do whatever You want to with me.
Be my Lord and Master.
Be my Lord and Master.
I open the door of my heart.
I open the door of my heart.
Here is my life.
Here is my life.
In Jesus' name.
In Jesus' name.
Amen.
Amen.

Lord, we believe that you have heard this because it has come from Ted's heart. And I pray, Lord, that you will help him to have the assurance that he really belongs to you. In Jesus' name. Amen.

C. Lead them through I John 5:11-13

I want to show you two or three verses here, Ted, and I'll be through. I think I see your bus coming over the hill. Read verse 11 out loud, please.

"And this is the record, that God has given to us eternal life, and this life is in His Son."   (I John 5:11)

In that verse, where is eternal life . . . according to that verse?

Where is it? It says it comes from God.

Look at verse 11 carefully. It says that eternal life is in . . . where?

In His Son, Jesus Christ. Eternal life is in Christ!

OK, eternal life is in Jesus Christ. Eternal life is not in the things that you do. It's not in church, though you might find out about it in church. It's not in the Bible, though you will find out about it in the Bible. Eternal life is in Jesus Christ. Now read verse 12 out loud, please.

"He that hath the Son hath life, and he that hath not the Son of God hath not life."

It says, he that has whom has eternal life?

The Son.

Who is the Son?

Jesus Christ.

He that has not Christ does not have eternal life. Ted, do you have Jesus Christ?

I do.

You opened your life to Jesus Christ and He has come in and you have Him. According to that verse, do you have eternal life?

Then I have eternal life. Yes!

You have given your life to whom, then?

Jesus Christ.

And how long will you belong to Him?

Forever!

Look at verse 13 there.

"These things have I written unto you that believe on the name of the Son of God, that ye may know that ye have eternal life." (I John 5:13)

It says, Ted that you can **know** you have eternal life. God's Word says it. Ted, you're no longer separated from God. You belong to Him. You're back now into that relationship for which you were made.

It all seems so easy. This is great! It all seems so clear to me.

Now listen, I'm going to give you a little book that I want you to read and I'm going to see you in a couple of days and see how you're coming. I know you will have a lot of questions. We went through a lot today, and I know you have a lot of questions about this. You know, one thing about this is you and I have the same Father—spiritually, that is. You and I are brothers, whether you like it or not, and we'll be together eternally.

Really?

I'm your older brother, spiritually, because you've just been—as the Bible says—"Born again." You are a spiritual baby. This means that I'm going to have to help you a little bit for the next few days. So I'll come by and see how you do on this little book—if you have any questions about it. Because you're a new baby, spiritually, you need to grow; you need to read the Bible and to talk with the Lord daily. And do this: when you see Tom this afternoon—you and Tom are pretty close, aren't you . . . ?

Yes.

You tell Tom what happened in your life. This will mean a lot to you. Remember this, you talk to Jesus Christ daily, and you let him talk to you through the Bible. This little book will help you. And then you tell somebody about it and I'll be talking to you later on.

Okay.

Here's your bus now. I'm sure glad it came a little late. 'Bye now!

Thanks, Jack, for talking with me. Nobody ever told me those things before. You know, I feel sorta different now . . . eh . . . 'bye . . . see you later.

FOLLOW-UP

A. Immediate Follow-up (Same day as profession)

By the way, Rene, happy birthday! The Bible says that when you placed your trust in the living Christ He caused you to be spiritually born anew. You have been "born again . . by the Word of God, which lives and abides forever."

Happy birthday
I Peter 1:23

Today is a very important day for you. Did you realize when you got up this morning that it would be your spiritual birthday? Because you have decided to trust Jesus Christ alone for your salvation you are now, in the deepest sense of the word, a member of the family of God.

It's good for that decision to be registered in black and white. This green card entitled "My Decision For Christ" is something I want to give to you as a reminder of what you have just done. Let's read it together:

Spiritual birth
certificate

> "My Decision For Christ." Knowing that I need the Lord Jesus Christ as my Saviour, I now trust Him to pardon and deliver me from the guilt and the power of sin.

> "As He gives me strength I shall witness for Him, serve Him in the fellowship of His church and seek to do His will in all areas of my daily life.

> > God said it . . . In His Word
> > I believe it . . . in my heart
> > That settles it . . . forever."

139

Let's put today's date here on this top line, and since this is your decision you sign on the next line.

On the back side I am writing my name, address and phone number. Contact me any time that I may be of assistance to you.

Keep this card in your billfold or purse. It is your spiritual birth certificate. It will help you remember that today you received new life, eternal life, and it can never be taken from you.

(Turn to Page 1, "Knowing Christ." The indented quotations are taken from the article "Your New Life.")

Facts of abundant life

"In the Gospel of John, we read that Christ said, 'My purpose is to give eternal life—abundantly!" God wants you to enjoy a full and vigorous life and has made provision for this. Here are some basic facts about this life.

The Bible Daily reading

"First, the Bible is food for the soul, which needs to be nourished just as your body does. Through His Word, God speaks to you and reveals His plan for your life—read the Gospel of John before reading any other book. Continue reading your Bible every day—try to read at least one chapter a day."

(Point out to the new Christian that the booklet in the front of the "Knowing Christ" package is actually The Gospel of John in the paraphrased Living New Testament translation.

The first part of this booklet is the Gospel according to John. It is written in modern English and is very easily understood.

STUDY I

(Turn to pages 3 through 5 and point out to them the two Bible studies.)
In this booklet you will also find two Bible studies.

It would be good to get started on these right away. Notice Bible Study I is entitled "The Savior and Eternal Life". All of the answers to the questions are found in the Gospel of John in the front of this packet. For example, notice question 1: "What did Jesus come into the world to do?" The answer to this question is found in John, chapter 1, verse 29. When we turn back to the gospel we find that John, chapter 1, verse 29 is on page 2. "The next day John saw Jesus coming toward him and said, Look! This is the Lamb of God who takes away the world's sin!" From this verse, what would you say is the answer to that question?

(Let him answer the question.)

Answer each of the questions in this same way. When you have finished Lesson No. 1, mail it to us in this envelope here in the back of the booklet. When we receive it, a second booklet entitled "Growing in Christ" will be sent to you. There is no charge for this and there is no obligation on your part. What we want is to see you grow as a Christian and be what God wants you to be.

When you have completed Bible Study I, begin on Bible Study II, "Promises In The Gospel of John." You will probably be able to have this second lesson completed by this time next week. It would be of value to you for us to go over it together. Is this same time and day next week all right for you or would there be a better time? If you have difficulty with the study, we can do it together.

(Set up your personal follow-up appointment at this time. Then turn back to page 1, "Your New Life" and continue with the article.)

"Prayer is your lifeline to God. Form the habit of starting each day with a few minutes in prayer. Conversation with God may seem strange at first, and you may be awkward and find it hard to know what to say. But as you continue, your prayers will become

"The Savior and eternal life"

STUDY II

"Promises in the Gospel of John"
(Personal follow-up appointment)

Prayer

141

more meaningful. So start each day with prayer, and then learn to pray throughout the day as the need arises. Take all of your problems and burdens to God, because He is interested in everything that you do. 'Casting all of your care upon him, for he careth for you.'

Witness

"Now that God has saved you, be His witness. You are to be an Ambassador for Him wherever you go. This doesn't mean that you go up and down the street telling everyone whom you meet. It does mean, however, that you start living a life that is different for your life is a big part of your witness. Then pray each day that you might share Christ with others, and God will open up opportunities. As you faithfully study and memorize the Scriptures, you will become better equipped to share Christ with others."

Witnessing is to your spiritual life what exercise is to your physical life. Without exercise the body becomes fat, flabby, and weak. Without sharing this gift of eternal life the spirit becomes sickly and powerless.

Mark 16:15
Acts 1:8
Luke 9:26

Jesus said, "Go into all the world and preach the Gospel to every living creature." He further said, "You shall receive power after the Holy Spirit comes upon you and you shall be witnesses unto me." In fact, Jesus went so far as to say, "Whosoever shall be ashamed of me and my words, of him shall the Son of Man be ashamed, when He shall come in His own glory and in His Father's, and of the holy angels."

(Training program)

We must tell others how they can receive this great gift. If you find this difficult, I will try to help you. We have a training program that can show you how to properly present the Gospel also.

Someone once said that this matter of witnessing

142

is simply the process of one beggar telling another beggar where he can find Bread.

"You can't be an effective Christian on your own. Take a full part in the life of your church. If you are not already a member, join a church where the Word of God is faithfully preached and taught. Pray for your minister, church officers, and teachers, that your church might make a strong impact in your community. Use your time and your money generously to help support the work of the church."

Church

When you cook with charcoal, you pile a number of charcoal briquettes together. When they get started, you spread them out and you can cook a feast fit for a king! But what can you do with one little coal all by itself? It hardly generates enough heat to warm a hot dog!

Solo Christians accomplish very little. The Apostle Paul said, "We, being many are one body in Christ, and everyone members one of another."

This is why the Bible warns us not to "forsake the assembling of ourselves together . . ."

Romans 12:5

Hebrews 10:25

If you feel you are in the church where God wants you to be, then be faithful to Him there. We who have received the gift of eternal life are all members of God's family. We are all members of the same Church, "the Church of the first born whose names are written in Heaven . . ." However, God puts each of us in a local church where we can best serve Him. Paul calls the church, "the body of Christ." We are members of that body. "God set the members every one of them in the body, as it has pleased Him." The only reason a person should leave one church and join another is because he is sure God wants him to.

Already active in another local church Hebrews 12:23

I Corinthians 12:18

If you have no active church home here, you

143

Not active in another local church

would be welcome in our next new members' class. The classes help a person know what it means to share in the ministry of our church. If you are interested in the next class I will ask one of the ministers to contact you.

This step you have taken does not mean that all your problems are automatically solved. In fact, you may find you have some new ones. You will **Satan** find that Satan, the enemy of your soul, will try to spoil the work that God is doing in you and will try to make you seriously doubt many things day by day. There is only one way to defeat him and that is through the Word of God. Follow the example of the Lord Jesus Christ when He was tempted in the wilderness. Each time Satan tempted Him, He quoted Scripture: "It is written."

Memorize Scripture

If Christ deemed it necessary to meet Satan with memorized Scriptures, then we too need to be able to meet temptation with Bible verses.

Psalm 119:11

Memorizing Bible verses will strengthen your spiritual life. The Word of God is alive and powerful. The psalm writer said, "Thy word have I hid in my heart that I might not sin against Thee." As you "hide" God's Word, not merely in your head but in your heart, He will give you power to live the full Christian life.

Someone has said, "God's Word will keep you from sin or sin will keep you from God's Word."

(Remove the Scripture memory cards from the back of the "Knowing Christ" packet. Separate them and place them in the envelope provided for them.)

These four promises will help you to withstand Satan's attacks and will strengthen your spiritual life. Begin by memorizing the promise of salvation. Then the promise of victory over temptation and

144

the promise of forgiveness and the promise of God's forgiveness.

Pages 7 through 12 explain the meaning of these promises. Read the explanation of the promises and it will help you memorize the verses.

Next week when we get together I would like for us to be able to recite from memory the first two promises.

When a child is born physically it is important that it grow. God has caused you to be spiritually born and now He commands you to "grow in the grace and knowledge of our Lord and Saviour, Jesus Christ." These four things: the Bible, prayer, witness, and worship through the church will help you to grow.

2 Peter 3:18a

(Turn to the list of instructions in the "Knowing Christ" packet.)

I know I've mentioned a number of things for you to do and you may be afraid that you will forget them. Each thing that I have said is listed here. Just check them off as you do them.

Instruction list

In order to help you to continue to grow another booklet like this will be sent to you through the mail every two weeks for the next six weeks.

Future booklets by mail

(Turn to the inside back page showing them the titles of the next three studies.)

These three studies Growing in Christ, Obeying Christ, Sharing Christ, will be sent to you without cost or obligation. Our desire is that you know Christ better and find the fullness of life which He has for each of us in the perfect center of His will.

I Corinthians 12:26

The Christian who ceases to grow hurts himself and the whole Christian church. "Whether one member suffers all the members suffer with it; or one member be honored, all the members rejoice with it." Each of us has the responsibility to grow as much as possible. Read Ephesians 4:11-16.

We must go now. By the way, which service will you be attending next Sunday morning? I'll look for you, and we can sit together. Once again, welcome to the family of God. I'll be back to see you next. . . . . at . . . . (a.m. or p.m.)

B. The New Testament New Christian Follow-up Program

I. Follow-up Defined

" . . . to be conformed (molded) to the image of His Son" (Romans 8:25) is the goal of all Christian nurture. Needless to say, the goal is more easily described than the pathway to the goal. We believe that the basic philosophy for Christian nurture is given by the Apostle Paul in I Thessalonians 2 in the similes of "a devoted mother nursing and cherishing her own children" (v.7), and "how like a father (dealing with) his children, we used to exhort each of you personally, stimulating, and encouraging, and charging you to live lives worthy of God . . ." (v. 11, 12 Amplified Bible). Therefore, all "nurture" activities—personal or group, pulpit or private—are designed with this basic philosophy in mind.

Christian lives are not mass produced

Henry Ford, the father of "mass production," is reported to have made the statement: "You can have any color Ford you want as long as it's black." His mass-producing manufacturing process required that everything be made exactly alike. While it is the goal of Christian nurture that each Christian be "Christ-like," we must keep in mind that Christian lives are not mass produced. It takes months instead of minutes to establish a lasting Christian

146

life . . . months (sometimes years) of pains-taking, "hot-house" nursery vigilance and care of the seeds sown and/or reaped by evangelism. To allow that when "one accepts Christ as Lord and Saviour he is constrained to spend himself in doing the work of Christ" and further to observe that "this work is to be done both as a member of a congregation and as an individual believer"[1] is one thing. It's another thing to get the "seedling" ready for such responsibilities. **"Short cuts in evangelism never work!"**[2] Mass production may work in building cars, but not in building Christians.

Short cuts in evangelism never work

To sum up, we have said that Christian nurture is a **process** of "training in righteousness (that is, in holy living, in conformity to God's will in thought, purpose and action), so that the man of God may be complete and profi-cient, well-fitted and thoroughly equipped for every good work." (Amplified Bible, II Timothy 3:16b—17). This training is life-long and en-compasses every phase of the church's work. Some call this process follow-up rather than Christian nurture, but we choose to say that follow-up applies only to the initial stages of the process, i.e., follow-up includes those im-mediate activities of nurture which begin at the time of decision, and continue until the "seedling" becomes a producing plant "doing the work of Christ."

Christian nurture is a process of "Training in Righteousness"

II. The Plan of Action
The New Testament, "New Christian" Follow-up Program follows a basic outline found in Waylon B. Moore's "New Testament Follow-up":[3]

---

[1]Presbyterian Church in the U.S., Inter-Agency Committee, General Council "Worship & Work of the Congregation." Atlanta: Presbyterian Church in the U.S., 1963.

[2]Presbyterian Church in the U.S., Division of Evangelism. "Workable Plan of Assimilation." Atlanta: Presbyterian Church in the U.S., n.d.

[3]Waylon B. Moore, ' New Testament Follow-Up" Wm. B. Eerdmans Co., 1963, p. 17.

Personal Follow-up
Consistent Follow-up
Church-Integrated Follow-up

Moore cites statistics which indicate that 95 percent of all Christian church members never win a soul to Christ. He further observes that 99 percent of those who are soul-winners never spend time in following up the souls they have won.[2]

The New Testament Evangelism Training Program at Coral Ridge is designed to reduce the former figure by training Christians to be soul-winners. The New Christian Follow-up Program purposes to reduce the latter by placing the responsibility for the vital incubator care of the "new babe" directly upon the initial soul winner (spiritual parent) and specific church groups (the spiritual family). In some cases, especially where sex may be a problem, it will be wise to have the new spiritual child adopted by another trained and mature Christian.

A. General Instructions

1. Duties of the Evangelist

   a. The Visitation Team Captain has the responsibility to fill out a Results Form for each day's visitation activity from visitors cards, and for each profession from an "Outside Call." Visitors' card is then stapled to the Results Form (see section on forms).

   b. On regular visitation day, when you plan to make a follow-up call, report to the church at the regular time for prayer and to pick up the materials you will need (See Section 2 below).

---

[2]Ibid., p. 19.

c. On follow-up calls, trainees should attend two follow-up calls during the course of their training (as observers). It is the trainer's responsibility to see that they receive this training in follow-up.

d. Personal support and encouragement by contact in the home and at church is important. The spiritual parent should maintain a healthy sense of responsibility for his spiritual child until that child is responsible for itself. This should form the background for all other follow-up work.

e. Seek to establish the new Christian in a Bible study group.

2. Materials Needed

a. Bible
b. A copy of Waylon B. Moore's "New Testament Follow-up"
c. "Knowing Christ" (Billy Graham)
d. "All Things Are Become New" (American Tract Society.
e. "Born to Reproduce" (The Navigators)

3. Schedule of Follow-up Contacts

Week	Activity
—	Profession—Immediate follow-up
Next day	Notify Undershepherd
1	Evangelist follow-up call
2	Mail "Growing In Christ"
3	Minister follow-up call on those not active in local church.
4	Mail "Obeying Christ"

　　　　　5　　　　Evangelist seeks to in-
　　　　　　　　　volve them in sharing
　　　　　　　　　group.
　　　　　6　　　　Mail "Sharing Christ"
　　　　　7　　　　Bible study group

4. Follow-up

Day of Profession
Assignment:
　　As detailed in "Knowing Christ"
　　and Immediate Follow-up Presen-
　　tation.

Evangelist Follow-up Call
　　To be made by Evangelist and
　　Trainee(s)

a. Procedure

　　　1. Ask the two questions.
　　　2. Go over Bible study II
　　　3. Recite the two memory verses:
　　　　　John 3:16 and I
　　　　　Corinthians 10:13

Evangelist Parental Responsibilities

The evangelist as the spiritual parent
is responsible to:
　　　1. Pray regularly by name for his
　　　　spiritual child.
　　　2. Maintain a personal support-
　　　　ive relationship with his spiri-
　　　　tual child.
　　　3. See that the other means of
　　　　follow-up are consistently ap-
　　　　plied to his spiritual child.
　　　4. Use every means available to
　　　　cause his spiritual child to be-
　　　　come a mature spiritual re-
　　　　producer. Encourage him to
　　　　enter the training program.

Ask him to be your trainee or find some other trainer with whom he will be comfortable.

5. If his spiritual child is not actively related to another church, he should encourage him to unite with his church and find his place of ministry in it.

Ministers Follow-up Call

The minister calls on those who have made professions and have no active relationship in a local church. This should be done after the follow-up call of the evangelist to be sure that the minister is using his time to the best advantage.

The purpose of this call is to become personally acquainted with the new Christian and to encourage him to become an active member in the church. This call can take the place of the contact with prospective new members during the class for membership.

First Group Bible Study
(Sharing Group)
Procedure

1. Spiritual parent picks up new Christian and takes him to Bible study group.
2. Commit follow-up to Bible study leader.
3. Maintain general oversight.

III. Personal Follow-up calls
George Sweazey has said, "The most healthy possible atmosphere for a new Christian is found in a warmly evangelistic church which is so enthusiastic about its faith that it is eager

151

to share it."[1] The warm atmosphere begins with the evangelistic visit. It begins when the evangelist says, "I have some Good News for you!" It continues when the evangelist asks, "Now isn't that the best news you ever received?" And it is furthered when the Christian finds this same excitement on the lips and in the lives and activities of the members of your church.

Being enthusiastic about your faith and being eager to share it means more than greeting a new Christian with a gleam in your eye, a smile on your lips, joy in your heart, a warm handclasp, and an effusive "Welcome to the family of God." It also involves practical activities designed to "feed" the new Christian. **A new Christian must not be left to shift for himself.** The obstetrician must be followed by the pediatrician. William J. McCullough sagely says, "I never saw a bassinet without sides."[2] Your task in follow-up is to put sides on the bassinet!

Overcome reluctance

You may be reluctant about making your first personal follow-up visit. That's natural. Satan gets mighty busy when someone steps out for Christ. But resist "the wiles of the devil."

The first follow-up visit should be scheduled into the regular calling program one week from the time of the profession. It also is wise to make contact by phone within three or four days after the profession.

One way to overcome your reluctance is to make arrangements for your first follow-up visit the same night the decision is made. Use the "Knowing Christ" Bible study lessons as your "return" bridge. Tell him you'll be back to go over the lesson with him. Once this date

---

[1]Geo. F. Sweazey, "Effective Evangelism," Harper & Row, 1953, p. 214.
[2]Ibid., p. 207.

is set—keep it!

The first follow-up visit is the time to nail down his **understanding** of the results of your evangelistic visit. Notice the words, "his understanding." You know what the "new babe" should understand, but your idea of what happened and his may be altogether different. Therefore we suggest you start the follow-up visit with the same two questions as the evangelistic visit, namely. (1) "Do you know if you have eternal life?", (2) "Why should God let you into heaven?" Another good question to get clarification of his understanding of your first visit is, "Mr.————————, if someone were to ask you how to become a Christian, what would you say?" The point is, don't assume he understands everything you said about trusting in Christ alone for salvation. Start your follow-up as a listener. Let him tell you what he knows. Ask your question; then hush-up and listen.

The first visit

Be a listener

A second phase of your first follow-up visit is to go over the lesson he has completed as assigned. Do this with a joyous, relaxed, but attentive manner. Listen for areas of possible misunderstanding, but refrain from leaping on these "to get him straightened out." Store them away for future instruction. Remember, he's probably reading the Bible for the first time in his life. He's not ready for your views on eschatology, soteriology, supralapsarianism versus infralapsarianism, or Pelagianism versus Augustinianism. Just be sure he understands in whom he is trusting for eternal life. **Don't stay too long on your first visit—an hour at most!** Always finish your visit with prayer.

This session will be welcomed by the new Christian if you pay attention to some basic considerations outlined by C. S. Lovett:

153

1. **Don't get off the subject.** Stay on target. Be objective in your discussions. Point to Christ. Don't use precious time to ventilate your personal feelings.

2. **Watch the time.** Don't impose. Keep your eyes on the clock. Be selective in dealing with questions. Don't get bogged down and use teaching time on unrelated things.

3. **Don't teach too fast.** A baby feeds from a bottle, not a fire hose.

4. **Don't give him too much.** Regardless of whether your new Christian seems to be a ready listener, refrain from giving too much at a time.

5. **Avoid controversial questions.** It has been well said that the mind of man can ask questions the mind of man can't answer, and that the answer may not be recognized by either questioner or answerer. (Dr. Gutzke, Columbia Seminary). Stay with the fundamentals of the faith . . . "the wayfaring men, though fools, shall not err therein." (Isaiah 35:8)

6. **Don't go unprepared.** "Study to show thyself approved unto God, a workman that needeth not to be ashamed, rightly dividing the Word of truth." (2 Tim. 2:15)

7. **Watch bad breath.** 'nuff said!

8. **Don't bring gloom into the convert's home.** Lay your burdens on the Lord and ask Him to fill you with the fruit of the Spirit. (Galatians 5:22)

9. **Don't teach with a "know-it-all" attitude.** Be positive in your teaching, not wishy-washy, maybe-so, but watch your attitude.

State your earnest convictions to yourself in front of a mirror and watch your expressions. You'll be glad you did.

10. **Don't argue.** See 2 Timothy 2 for help on this point.[1]

You should stress that personal Bible reading and study is "good" for a new Christian to do. It will feed him. Care should be exercised that you don't burden him with the thought that the whole Bible must be read within the week. Don't recommend that he start with Genesis and read straight through.

Encourage Bible reading

Point out that the Bible is a "library" of 66 books, and that certain of these books are more helpful than others for a new Christian. (Who would recommend that a person who has just learned to read start with the "A" index file in a city library and read straight through!) Suggest the following order: The Gospel of John, then Romans, then the New Testament. The Gospel of John which has verses underlined to encourage him to follow a consecutive thought pattern regarding the good news he has received is excellent (Pocket Testament League or Living New Testament).

Subsquent visits should be social and sharing visits. Maintain contact so that you can encourage and support him. Invite him to your home for dinner. Try to attend the same morning service and introduce him to other members. Don't come on too strong but prayerfully seek to cause him to feel at home in the family of God. Also encourage him to complete the correspondence studies.

IV. Group Follow-up

Personal follow-up calls should pave the way

---

[1] C. S. Lovett, "Follow-up Made Easy," The Lockman Foundation, 1957, pp. 46-49.

to deeper Bible study in small groups.

A. The following are suggestions on how to motivate your new Christian's interest and enlist him into a group.

    1. On Evangelist's follow-up call, explain Bible study groups and ask them to make plans to give one hour each week to meeting with such a group.

    2. Check with the Evangelism Secretary to obtain at least two Bible study group meeting times.

    3. By the fifth week after the profession arrange to take him to the first meeting of the Bible study group and introduce him to group and leader.

    4. Follow the attendance of the contact during the course of the Bible study.

    5. If a new Christian drops out of a Bible study group, the Group Leader should contact the person who did the original follow-up for assistance in recruiting the "backslider."

    6. When a Bible study group has completed a unit of study they may elect to continue with another unit, or (as is preferred) they may each become a leader in a new Bible study group.

Consistent follow-up is conducted through a program of Cell-Group Bible Study. The Navigators' "Studies in Christian Living," Billy Graham Group Studies, or Growth by Groups series are study source books. The booklets are well planned and well written. Their contents carefully balance a truly objective view concerning the teaching of the Bible and the problems of subjective introspection which can bog a group down.

B. Procedure For Cell Groups

1. The study group is recruited from those who make professions of faith. Each evangelist is aware of such classes and encourages the new Christian to participate. (This study class follows the personal follow-up visits.)

2. The class is restricted to 6—8 members.

3. The leader of the group does not need to be a "Bible scholar," but a person who is willing to keep the discussion to the point.

4. Refreshments may or may not be served but this should not be part of the one-hour study time.

5. The group meets for one hour only.

6. Each member of the group must prepare the lesson.

7. The hour for the meeting must be agreeable for all.

8. The cell group should divide after about six months. (The participants in cell groups are excellent for future leaders.)

9. Leaders of cell groups will find the "Outline For Leading Bible Study Groups" helpful.

C. Leading Bible Study Groups—Outline

1. The Job of the Leader

There are three stages to successful Bible study. They are discovery, understanding, and application. The job of the leader is to guide the group members into their own discovery of the message of the Scriptures and then to help them comprehend the implications of these discoveries and then, finally, from this to encourage each one to make the personal applications that will shape his life.

The leader stimulates and guides. He does not lecture. He does not have to be a Great Bible Scholar. In fact, he doesn't have to know much about the Bible at all.

2. Preparation for the Discussion

A. The leader is the pacesetter. As such his personal standard for preparation should exceed the standard that he sets for the rest of the group. Leader, be thorough in your personal study preparation **You will be followed** and the success of the study depends on the personal preparation of the other group members.

B. Prepare the questions you will use in conducting the discussion in advance. Prepare three types of questions.
   1. Launching questions—to open discussion on a subject.
   2. Guide questions—to maintain the course of the discussion.
   3. Summary questions—to consolidate what has been discussed.

C. Pray for each member of the study group.

3. Conducting the Discussion

A. Provide opportunity to report on how the application from last week's study went. What effects were noted? What problems occurred?
B. Open discussion with launching questions. Sustain and direct with guide and summary questions.
C. Avoid tangents. When the discussion strays, enter with a summary of what has been said and redirect the discussion with a question of your own.
D. Draw out the silent ones and control the verbose.
E. Keep your own talking to a minimum—one-third of the time or less.
F. End by discussing the applications that are being drawn for the following week.

G. Watch the time of the discussion. It is inexcusable to bore people with the Bible. Don't plod through every verse. There is a lot of ground to cover in every study, so cover the most relevant, eliminating the rest.

D. Church-Integrated Follow-up

The problem of assimilating new members is reduced by the many follow-up activities already discussed. But it still remains. Not all who come into the church are the results of the evangelism program. Those who do come into the church through evangelism and are not able to receive the same intense personal follow-up are encouraged to join in the same program.

1. Invitation for Membership

Members are received on a quarterly schedule. Invitations are given by the pastor from the pulpit, in the bulletins, and of course by the spiritual parents. (Care must be exercised by the spiritual parent not to give the impression that his only interest in the new Christian is church membership.) Those who are interested are asked to fill in an application for membership and return it to one of the pastors.

Invite to join

2. Pastor's Visit

Prior to or during the time of "membership classes" (see below) the pastor visits each one who has filled in an application for membership. This is a MUST. The purpose is twofold: For the pastor to get acquainted, and more importantly, for the pastor to determine where the individual is "spiritually." The pastor's visit takes much the same form as the first follow-up visit described above. Let us stress again. This vist is a MUST. It is done before any new member is received. **We believe that the careful, private investigation of an individual's spiritual understanding of his faith by the pastor is the most important step you can take in building a spiritual church.** You should allow two hours for this visit.

Pastor's visit

3. Membership Classes

Those who are interested in membership are invited and exhorted to attend membership classes conducted by the senior pastor. We hold such classes for one hour following the Sunday evening service for four weeks. These classes are not compulsory but we do stress their helpfulness to the individual's familiarity with the church, her beliefs and activities. The subject matter is:

Class I. Doctrine

      a. What all Christian churches believe in common
      b. What all Protestant churches believe in common

Class II. Doctrine—What our church believes

Class III. Sacraments and Church Government

Class IV. Basic Christian Duties

      a. Scripture reading
      b. Prayer
      c. Church attendance
      d. Stewardship—time, talents, possessions
      e. Witnessing

Plenty of time is allowed for answering questions, but don't get bogged down in the meeting. Make personal appointments where you see the need to discuss touchy points with individuals. Due to your evangelism program you may expect to have people from varied backgrounds. The classes outlined will be a great help in clarifying many confusing things for them.

4. Membership Day

The keynote for membership day is **make it meaningful.** We follow this procedure.

a. The group meets with the church officers before the 11 a.m. Sunday

160

service. They are received as new members either by profession of their faith, reaffirmation of their faith, or transfer of their church letter. This information has been determined by the pastor on his visit. The individuals are carefully catalogued so that proper acknowledgment may be made when they are introduced to the congregation.

b. Each individual in the group is introduced and called to come forward at the 11 a.m. service. When the group is formed, the pastor reads the membership procedure from the manual, asks the questions, and welcomes the new members.

c. Following the Sunday evening service, a reception is held in honor of the new members. Every effort is made to warmly welcome the new members. It should be a "day to be remembered."

5. Assimilating New Members

The third now of follow-up is assimilating new members. This means giving careful attention to help new members form lasting friendships and become a part of the work of the church. Sweazey well warns that "not having seen each other for a week, they (the old members) give newcomers a brief nod and eagerly get on with the communion of saints . . . if left to the natural laws of social life, the assimilation of new members is not likely to take place at all. Therefore, churches find it necessary to make special provisions for it."[1]

Assimilate new members

---

[1]Sweazey, op. cit., p. 232.

6. New Members Sponsors

After new members have been received
into the church, their names are assigned
to mature members who agree to be their
sponsor for a period of three months. Assignments are made by a committee of
three members who are well acquainted
with the congregation. Tentative assignments should be made as soon as membership is applied for. All assignments
should be checked with the minister before
actually being made. Letters of final assignment should be mailed as soon as the
members are received by the official board.
A copy of the application for membership
or something similar can be given to the
sponsor to acquaint him with his new
member.

A system of records showing who is sponsoring whom is important. It is also important that sponsors be sponsored by an
officer of the church or a pastor. During
the three month period that they serve
they should meet at least twice to share
the results of their sponsoring activities.
A check list enclosed in the sponsor letter
should be turned in by each sponsor on
each new member.

The following letter and check list out-
lining sponsor responsibilities to the new
member and his family is sent to each
sponsor.

Comments:

SPONSORS CHECK LIST

NEW MEMBER

Name_____

Address_____

Phone No._____

Check the following items as you do them. This list is to be turned in at the first Sponsor's Meeting.

☐ 1. Pray for them daily by name.

☐ 2. Welcome them personally as new members.

☐ 3. Call on them in their homes. Be observant and note any interesting features about their home which will help you to know them better. Notice books and magazines, and any hobby indications.

   4. Find out which morning service they are attending. Greet them at the church and introduce them to others. You may want to come to church together or sit together for the next few Sundays. When the member misses a service you should telephone—not as a truancy officer—but to inquire whether there is illness and to express regret that you did not see each other.

☐ 5. Invite them to attend the evening service with you.

☐ 6. Try to get the new member into church organizations and activities, perhaps arranging to go together or prodding an organization if it is negligent in its recruiting. Your relationship to the new member will help bridge the gap between joining the church and enlistment into its total ministry.

☐ 7. Give him an invitation to your home and/or arrange for social occasions at the homes of other church members.

☐ 8. Discover and try to use the new member's talents in the ministry of the church.

☐ 9. Give such guidance in Christian living as can be tactfully offered, i.e., suggestions for family and personal devotions.

☐ 10. Watch for any sign of failure to get a good start and try to correct it—calling on others to help as needed and notifying the pastors immediately if there are problems or difficulties you cannot handle.

Community Church

495 MAIN STREET
ANYTOWN, USA

DR. JOHN JONES
MINISTER

Dear John Doe:

You have been selected to be a sponsor for one of our new members.

The first 90 days in the life of a new member are most critical! It is important that they be made to feel that they are a part of the church family and that they find their place of service in the ministry of the church.

As a sponsor you will be expected to do the things listed on the enclosed New Member Sponsor Check List.

On Sunday, February 8, at 5:30 p.m.,* we would like for you to meet with all the other sponsors of new members in the church Fellowship Hall. At that time you will be able to share the problems and the joys you have encountered. Also at this meeting you will be asked to turn in your "Sponsor Check List" indicating what you have done with your new member.

I am enclosing a copy of a letter which was recently sent to each new member.

This is a silent service. The new member does not know that you are his sponsor. However, if he should ask you if you were assigned to him, tell him we do this with all new members so that they may quickly and meaningfully become a part of the church family.

If for some reason you are not able to serve as a sponsor of the person here named, notify me immediately.

Let me underscore again the importance of your relationship to the new member. Call me for any assistance I can provide.

Sincerely in Christ,

Minister of Visitation

---

*Sponsors should meet twice during the 90-day period.

7. New Members Class Socials

As soon as possible following official reception of new members there should be
a class get-together. This provides an
opportunity for new members to become
acquainted with each other in a way that
is not possible during the periods of instruction. The new members may share in
a pot-luck dinner or the church may provide a buffet or a coffee and dessert.
Workers related to various church activities are present to acquaint the new members with specific program opportunities.
After a time of getting acquainted—when
each person states his name, where he is
from, his occupation and family status,
there is a time of spiritual sharing. Individuals at random tell how they came to
know Christ and the results of Him being
in their life.

The meeting is closed with a time of prayer
and with the word that there will be a similar gathering three months hence at which
time each new member will be asked (1)
How is the church meeting your needs?
and (2) How are you fitting into the ministry of the church?

A second get-together is scheduled for
three months after the new member has
been received. This is started with a coffee
and dessert and is followed by discussion
of the two questions announced at the
first social. Each new member is asked to
put on paper his answers to the two questions.

8. The Undershepherding Program

Undershepherds are men who are spiritually mature and their wives. The under-

shepherd is responsible for calling in the homes of those in his group. He also has them in his home on a quarterly basis. The purpose of this is to keep direct contact with every member of the church. Each new member is assigned to an undershepherding group. Undershepherds are notified when there is a Christian in his area who is attending church but has not yet joined the church. He is to pass this information on to his 'flock'.

9. New Members Class

This class is held at the Sunday school hour for 8—10 weeks. It is taught by one of the pastors, an elder, or a qualified teacher along the same lines as outlined in the Bible study class.

10. Women of the Church—Circles

11. Men of the Church

12. Mid-week School of the Bible

13. Sunday School Teacher Training

14. Special Weekly Bible Classes (Minister of Education)

15. Choir

16. Boy Scouts or Christian Service Brigade

17. Girl Scouts or Pioneer Girls

18. Youth Activities

19. Evangelism

20. Other Special Activities

a. Bible Memory Groups

It is fun to memorize Scripture when it's done in a group. The Navigators have a Topical Memory Course which can be used to structure your efforts. We have found that a sense of competition adds flavor if teams are chosen to check each others' weekly "memory work." This is an excellent way to get men together during the week. They can grab a sandwich and milkshake and meet for lunch at the church or some other convenient location. Here again, be sure a strong leader is on hand to guide the discussions. This is also a good time for the pastor to have fellowship with others.

b. Prayer Partners

It goes without saying that one of the best ways to show enthusiasm about your faith is to pray. Encourage your new Christian to seek the Lord with you in prayer. He will be hesitant at first, but by your example you can lead him into his most meaningful spiritual times in prayer.

c. Circles of Concern

The women's circles of our church instituted a program for praying for the spiritual growth and understanding for each new Christian. Their idea does two things: It strengthens the new Christian to know that people are praying for him, and it stimulates the zeal of the members of the circles as they see God at work in bringing men and women to Himself. Each new Christian's name is given to a chairman.

**Memorize
Scripture**

Pray

She in turn assigns one of the circles to pray for him.

d. Evangelism Training

Many new Christians are anxious to share the Good News they have received with others. At our church training in evangelism is going on throughout the year. The evangelist who is working with his new Christian is the logical one to support his interest in telling others and to introduce him to the training available. The spiritual parent may not be the best one to train him but he sees that he gets the training.

CARD FORMS

SAMPLE ROLODEX CARD

```
Jones, M/M John A. (Mary)          1-1-69
6972 S.W. 57 St.                   1-15-69
Ft. L.       566-2239              2-16-69
Here until May
Baptist, Detroit
1/10/69—Christians. Susan Smith
```

SAMPLE WORSHIPER REGISTRATION CARD
(PRINTED ON TWO COLOR STOCK TO FACILITATE SORTING)

WELCOME TO OUR VISITORS

. . . . .PRESBYTERIAN CHURCH

Please fill out this card and place it in the offering plate.

NAME _____

LOCAL ADDRESS   SIDE 1

   Street _____   WHITE

   City _____ Tel. No. _____

Permanent Resident _____ or Here until _____

Home Church _____

Desire a local church home _____ Request a call _____

My age is _____ Grades 1-3 _____ Junior High _____ 18-24 _____ 41-55

            _____ Grades 4-6 _____ High School _____ 25-40 _____ Over 55

THE . . . . PRESBYTERIAN CHURCH

MEMBER REGISTRATION

(Visitors Please Use Other Side)

NAME _____   SIDE 2

   Message to Pastors . . . Change of Address . . . Prayer Request . . .   BLUE

       New Residents in Your Area

_____

_____

_____

RESULTS FORM

Date _____ 19____ AM_____ PM_____ Visitor Card _____or Outside Call_____

Result (use Code above)_____ (If Follow Up) Step # _____ Number of houses where no one was home:_____

Did you record "NH" & Date on back of Visitor cards for those who were not at home?

Yes_____   No_____

Name Called On _____

Address _____ City_____

Member of local church? Yes_____ No_____; What church?_____ Occupation or

profession_____ Approx. age_____ Marital Status_____

Listeners in the Home _____

Name of Evangelist _____

Others on Team _____

Profession Only:

Name of Person making profession_____

Appointment made for follow-up next week? (yes or no) Wednesday am_____

   Thursday pm_____ Other day_____ Date_____ Time_____

Did you leave "Knowing Christ" and assign Lessons: Yes_____ No_____

Christian Only:

Name of Christian _____

Comments _____

_____

_____

_____

_____

_____

_____

_____

_____

_____

_____

_____

_____

_____

_____

_____

_____

PROF	—	Gospel presented, profession made	N H	—	Found no one at home
GPND	—	Gospel presented, no decision	NO ADM	—	No admittance—would not let us in
REJ	—	Gospel presented, rejected	FR V	—	Just a friendly visit
GPA	—	Gospel presented for assurance	FOL UP	—	Made a follow-up call
XN	—	Already a Christian	TEST	—	Personal testimony only given

EVANGELIST ACTIVITY CARD

NAME _____ PHONE _____

ADDRESS _____ CITY _____

Date training was completed (Gospel presented for first time.) _____

Trainees (1) _____ (2) _____ (3) _____

(4) _____ (5) _____ (6) _____

Inactive (date) _____ Reason: _____

Returned (date) _____ Reason: _____

Date	Code	Name of Profession	Visitor Card or Outside Call	Name of Evangelist	Others on Team	Step Completed

PROF — Gospel Presented, PROFESSION Made		N H — Found NO ONE at HOME
GPND — Gospel Presented, NO DECISION		NO ADM — NO ADMITTANCE would not let us in
REJ — Gospel Presented, REJECTED		FR V — Just a FRIENDLY VISIT
GPA — Gospel Presented for ASSURANCE		FOL UP — Made a FOLLOW-UP Call
XN — Already a CHRISTIAN		TEST — Personal TESTIMONY Only Given

FOLLOW-UP LEDGER

Name of Profession _____ Phone_____

Address _____City_____

Name of Evangelist_____Others on Team_____

Date of Profession _____19_____Visitor's Card_____or Outside Call_____

Dropped out of Follow-up Program (date) _____19_____ Reason: _____

Step No.	Date	Description	Comments
1		Form to Undershepherd	
2		Evangelist follow-up call	
3		Mail: "Growing in Christ" (2 wks.)	
4		Minister Follow-up Call	
5		Mail: "Obeying Christ" (4 wks.)	
6		Mail: "Sharing Christ" (6 wks.)	
7		New Member Class Letter	
8		Bible Study Group	

Visitation Procedure Before the Visit

1. Members and visitors fill out cards in pews on Sunday.

2. Office separates Visitors Cards from Members Cards.

3. Members attendance posted to attendance records.

4. Notify by post card undershepherds when one of their flock misses more than three consecutive Sundays.

5. Separate out-of-town from local visitors.

6. Send postal card to out-of-state.

7. File alphabetically under zip codes.

8. Annual letter inviting visitor back to the church and informing them of current ministry.

9. Destroy out-of-town cards.

10. Alphabetize local Visitors Cards.

11. Check Rolodex File to see if visitors have attended previously.

12. Post-date to Rolodex card the visitors who have attended before.

13. Destroy these Visitors Cards.

14. Make up Rolodex Card for first-time visitors (those who do not have a card in the Rolodex file.)

15. File Rolodex card.

16. Post neighborhood code to first-time Visitors Cards.

17. Look up phone number; post to Visitors Card and Rolodex.

18. Call each Visitors Card for appointment.

19. Give those indicating they desire a local church home to ministers.

20. Sort Visitors Cards by neighborhood code for non-appointments.

21. Group Visitors Cards by neighborhood code; 3 to 5 per packet.

22. Hand out appointments and packets at Visitation.

23. Teams go out on Visitation and report back to church after visit is completed.

VISITATION PROCEDURE   BEFORE THE VISIT

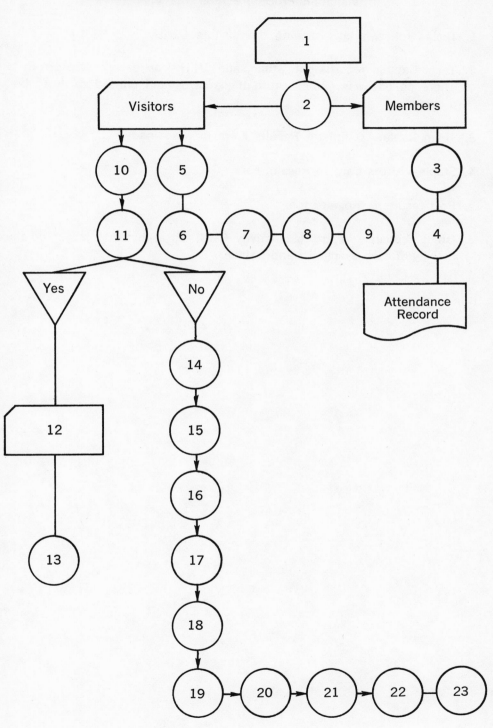

Visitation Procedure After the Visit

1. Teams return from visit with the Visitors Cards.

2. Team Captain records date, time, and "N.H." on back of Visitors Card where no one was home; return these cards and unused cards to box provided.

3. Team Captain completes Results Form for visit made.

4. Staple Visitors Card to Results Form.

5. Post results to Rolodex file.

6. Office prepares "Evangelist Activity Card" as a complete ledger on the activity of each evangelist and trainee.

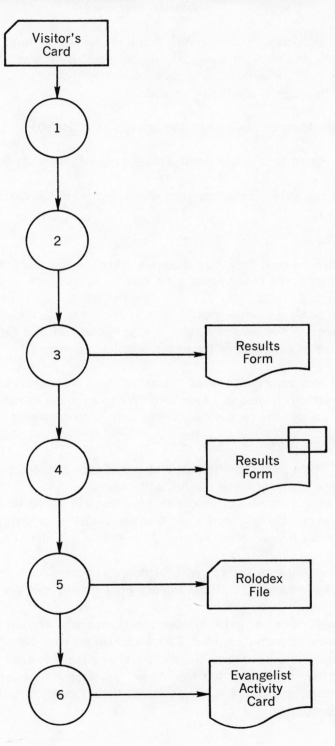

Follow-up Procedure

1. Team captains (trainer) complete the proper results form when returning to the church from their call. If the result code was "Profession", or Christian", a white form is completed. For "Follow-up", "No Decision", or "Rejection", a yellow form is used.

2. Separate results forms into five groups as indicated.

3. The 3-part results form is separated by the Evangelism Secretary.

4. The Evangelism Secretary gives the pink form to the Undershepherd Secretary.

5. Undershepherd Secretary prepares a pink name and address strip for placing in the geographical strip file.

6. The pink copy of the results form is mailed to the undershepherd living closest to the person making the profession so that he can notify the others in his group of the new profession's presence.

7. The blue copy of the results form for those making professions who are not actively related to a local church is given to the minister. The minister will contact the person making the profession regarding church membership.

8. The office uses the white copy of the results form to create a Follow-up Ledger Card for those making professions.
   Three successive correspondence studies (1) "Growing in Christ", (2) "Obeying Christ", and (3) "Sharing Christ" are mailed in two-week intervals following the creation of the Follow-up Ledger Card.

9. Office prepares a 3 x 5 yellow follow-up address card which is given to the team captain for use in making his follow-up call the following week.

10. Results forms of those making professions who are not actively related to local churches are filed. Two weeks before each New Members Class, a letter of invitation to the membership classes is sent to each person who has a form in this file. When "professions" become members or indicate no interest in membership, their forms are transferred to file in Step 11.

Follow up Procedure

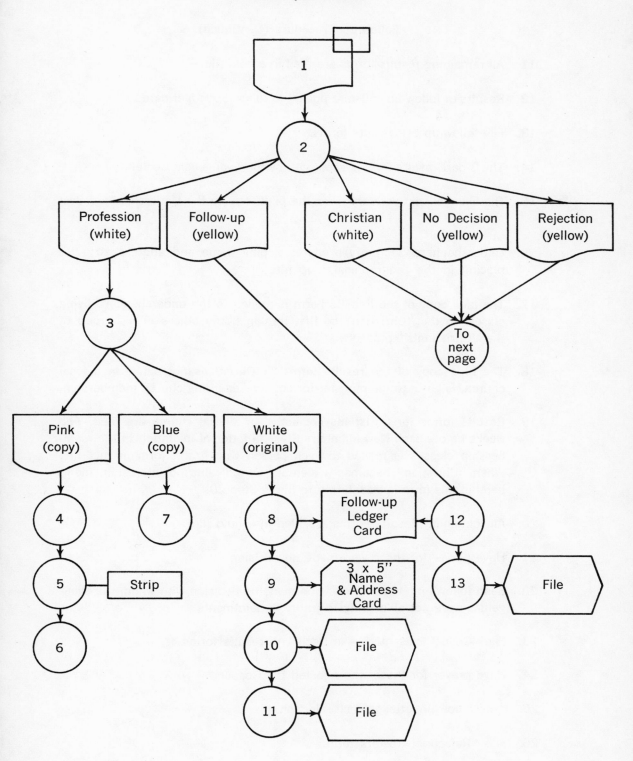

Follow-up Procedure (Continued)

11. All remaining results forms are filed in a hold file.

12. Results of follow-up calls are posted to follow-up ledger cards.

13. File follow-up call results forms.

14. The 3-part results form is separated by the Evangelism Secretary.

15. The Evangelism Secretary gives the pink form to the Undershepherd Secretary.

16. Undershepherd Secretary prepares a pink name and address strip for placing in the geographical strip file.

17. The pink copy of the Results Form is mailed to the undershepherd living closest to the "Christian" so that he can notify others in his group of the "Christian's" presence.

18. The blue copy of the results form, for Christians not active in a local church, is given to the minister for contact regarding church membership.

19. Results forms for Christians not active in a local church are filed. Two weeks before each New Members Class, a letter of invitation to the membership classes is mailed to each person who has a form in this file. When "Christian" becomes a member or indicates no interest in membership, his form is transferred to file in Step 20.

20. All remaining Results Forms are filed in a hold file.

21. Have prayer for those who made no decision.

22. Send follow-up letter to those who made no decision with whom the evangelists were not able to make future appointments.

23. File "Gospel Presented—No Decision" results forms.

24. Have prayer for those who rejected the Gospel.

25. Send follow-up letter to each rejection.

26. File "Rejection" results form.

Follow-up Procedure (Continued)

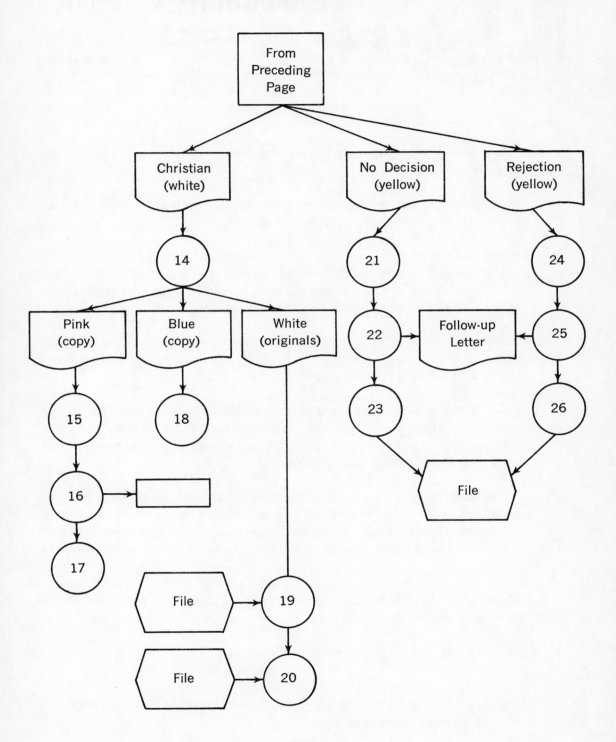

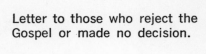

Community Church

495 MAIN STREET
ANYTOWN, USA

DR. JOHN JONES
MINISTER

Dear _____,

Thank you for the hospitality extended to the members of our church who recently visited you.

We appreciated the opportunity to share the Good News of God's gift of Eternal Life even though you did not at that time receive the gift.

It may seem hard to believe that something this great can be so simply and easily obtained, but incredible as it may appear it is true! God declares that He "loved the world so much that he gave his only Son so that anyone who believes in Him will not perish but have eternal life."

In the light of this offer of love, God says there can be no neutrality. Jesus declared, "He that is not with me is against me." To make no decision for Jesus Christ is in reality a rejection of Him.

If His love is refused, it one day may be totally withdrawn. God says in His word that the Lord Jesus Christ will come again and do justice upon those who obey not the Gospel. They will suffer the punishment of eternal ruin, cut off from the presence of the Lord forever.

If you have not already received this greatest of all gifts, please do it now. In-dicate this decision on the enclosed postage-free card and a booklet explaining the full meaning of the gift of eternal life will be sent to you without cost or obligation. Any questions relating to this subject may be written on the enclosed card.

We hope that you will continue to worship with us. Feel free to call on me if I may be of any service to you.

Sincerely,
Visitation Minister

P.S. The enclosed folder contains a summary of the Good News of God's Gift of Eternal Life and how to receive it.

Enclosure referred to in letter to those who reject the Gospel or make no decision.

THE GOOD NEWS

1. Eternal life (Heaven) is the free gift of God.
   "The free gift of God is eternal life."
   Romans 3:23
   It is not earned or deserved.
   "It is the gift of God; not of works lest any man should boast."
   Ephesians 2:8, 9
2. We are sinners and cannot save ourselves.
   "All have sinned and come short of the glory of God." Romans 3:23
3. God loves us and does not want to punish us.
   "Yes, I have loved you with an everlasting love." Jeremiah 31:3
   God is just and must punish our sin.
   "Righteousness and justice are the foundation of thy throne."
   Psalms 89:14
   "I will visit their transgression with the rod and their iniquity with stripes." Psalms 89:32
4. God became man in the person of Jesus of Nazareth.
   "In the beginning was the word, and the word was with God, and the word was God . . . and the word became flesh and dwelt among us."
   John 1:1, 14
   He lived a perfect life and by his death paid the penalty for our sins.
   "He who knew no sin, he made to be sin on our behalf."
   II Corinthians 5:21
   "While we were yet sinners, Christ died for us." Romans 5:8
   Jesus was raised from the dead so that he might give us eternal life (Heaven).
   "Jesus was raised for our justification." Romans 4:25

5. We receive the gift of eternal life by faith.
   Faith is not merely mental assent.
   "You believe there is one God; you do well: The demons also believe and tremble." James 2:19
   Nor is faith the confidence expressed in our daily life in God's care for our temporal needs.
   "The things which are seen are temporal; but the things which are not seen are eternal."
   II Corinthians 4:18
   Faith that enables us to receive the gift of eternal life is trusting Jesus Christ alone for the salvation of our immortal souls.
   "He that believes on the Son has eternal life; but he that believes not the Son shall not see life but the wrath of God abides on Him."
   John 3:36
   "In none other is there salvation for neither is there any other name under heaven, that is given among men wherein we must be saved."
   Acts 4:12
   Jesus seeks entrance into the control center of our lives.
   Jesus said, "I stand at the door and knock: if any man hear my voice, and open the door, I will come in to him." Revelation 3:20
   God gives us eternal life (Heaven) when we say to him, "I am sorry for my sin. I wish to turn from it and to trust in you alone for the salvation of my soul. I willingly give to you the controls of my life."

1.

2.

This is the Good News of God's free gift of eternal life (Heaven) to those who trust in Jesus Christ alone. To those who receive this gift, Jesus says, "Truly, truly, I say unto you, he that believes on me has everlasting life." John 6:47

If you have any questions on heaven and eternal life contact:

THE

GOOD NEWS

New Membership Procedure

1. Three orientation classes

2. Applicant interviews with minister unless previously interviewed.

3. Acceptance by Church Board.

4. Public recognition.

5. Sponsor assigned to new member.

6. New member assigned to Undershepherd Group.

7. First New Members Class social gathering.

8. New Members 8—10 week Sunday school Class.

9. Second New Members Class social gathering.

10. Personal invitation to join in evangelism program as a trainee.

CHURCH MEMBERSHIP PROCEDURE

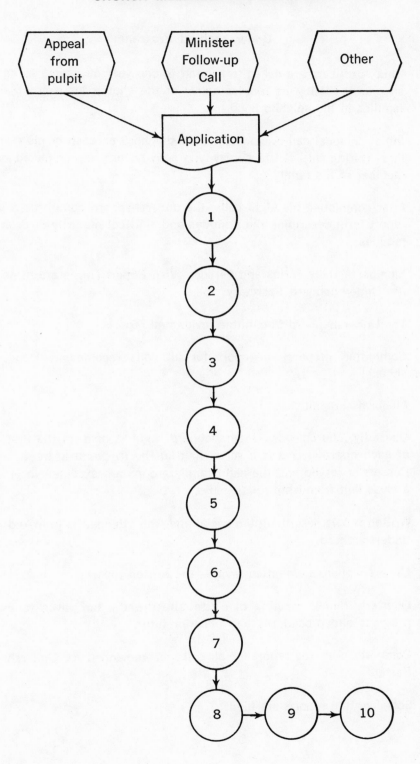

Undershepherd Program

1. Church officers are asked to commit to one year of service as an under-shepherd. (Acting as representative of the church for a group of eight families in his neighborhood.)

2. Initial personal call is made by undershepherd on each of his eight families. During this call, a survey-type activity form is completed on each member of the family.

3. After completing his eight calls, the undershepherd completes a general report form describing the attitudes and spiritual maturity of each of his families.

4. Member Activity Forms and Personal Visit Report Forms are turned in to the Undershepherd Secretary.

5. The Undershepherd Committee reviews all reports.

6. Committee prepares a report for all calls recommended for under-shepherd.

7. All forms are filed.

8. Quarterly, church-wide, Undershepherd Night is held on the first Friday of each quarter. This is a social held at the undershepherd's home. Dessert is served and the eight family groups are expected to grow into a close knit friendship relationship.

9. Written report describing the social and who attended is prepared by the undershepherd.

10. Undershepherd Committee reviews the written reports.

11. Quarterly dinner meeting of undershepherds and wives to evaluate progress and procedures and plan for future.

12. Committe prepares report for all calls recommended for Undershepherd Pastor.

13. Social written reports are filed.

UNDERSHEPHERD PROGRAM

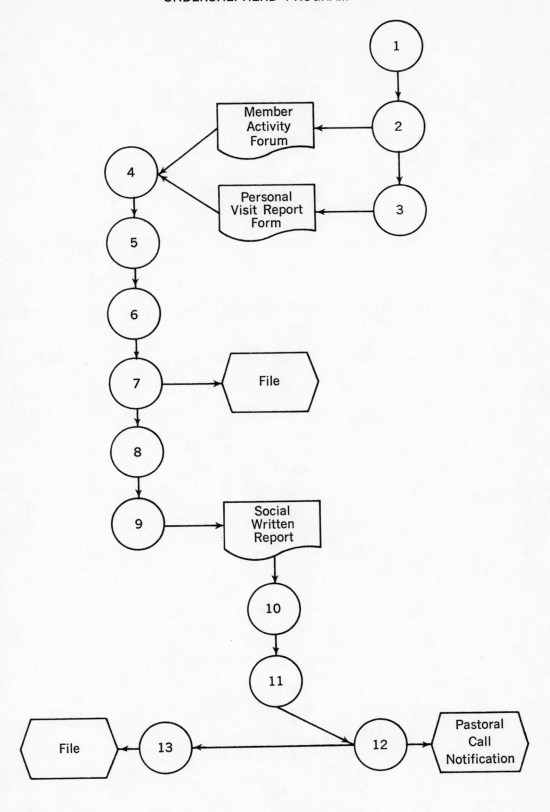

Bibliography

Allan, Tom; The Face of My Parish; Harper & Row; 1953

Allen, Roland; The Spontaneous Expansion of the Church; World Dominion Press; 1940

Allen, Roland; Missionary Methods: St. Paul's or Ours; World Dominion Press; 1953

Augsburger, Myron S.; Invitation to Discipleship; Herald Press; 1964

Autrey, C. E.; Evangelism in the Acts; Zondervan; 1964

Autrey, C. E.; Basic Evangelism; Zondervan; 1959

Barclay, William; Fishers of Men; Westminster; 1966

Barrett, E. P.; Sunday School Evangelism; Evangelical Teacher Training Association; 1966

Baxter, Richard; A Call to the Unconverted; Zondervan; 1963

Bonar, Horatius; Words to Winners of Souls; American Tract Society; reprint 1962

Boston, Thomas; Art of Man-Fishing; Sovereign Grace; 1964

Bryan, Dawson C.; Building Church Membership Through Evangelism; Abingdon; 1962

Burns, James; Revivals, Their Laws and Leaders; Baker; 1960

Caemmerer, Richard R.; The Church and the World; Concordia; 1949

Chafin, Kenneth; Help! I'm a Layman; Word Books; 1966

Chirgiven A. M.; The Bible in World Evangelism; Friendship Press; 1954

Coleman, Frank G.; The Romance of Winning Children; Union Gospel Press; 1967

Coleman, Lyman; Growth by Groups; Christian Outreach

Coleman, Robert E.; Dry Bones Can Live Again; Revell; 1969

Coleman, Robert E.; The Master Plan of Evangelism; Revell; 1968

Crawford, Percy B.; The Art of Fishing for Men; Moody; 1950

Dobbins, Gaines S.; Winning the Children; Broadman; 1953

Dixon, Amzi; Glories of the Cross; Eerdmans; 1962

Edwards, E. Henry and Whitesell, Faris D.; Sowing Gospel Seed; Moody; 1954

Ellis, Hallett W.; Fishing for Men; Zondervan; 1955

Ewin, Wilson; You Can Lead Roman Catholics to Christ; Christian Publications; 1964

Finney, Charles; Revival Lectures; Revell

Ferm, Robert O.; Psychology of Christian Conversion; Revell, 1959

Ford, Leighton; The Christian Persuader; Harper & Row; 1966

Fuller, David O.; Valiant for the Truth; Lippincott; 1961

Gager, LeRoy; Handbook for Soul-Winners; Zondervan; 1956

Gartenhaus, Jacob; Winning Jews to Christ; Zondervan; 1963

Green, Bryan; The Practice of Evangelism; Scribner; 1957

Grubb, Norman P.; Continuous Revival; Christian Literature Crusade

Harrison, Eugene M.; How to Win Souls; Scripture Press; 1952

Haskins, Dorothy C.; Soul-Winning; Baker; 1959

Hayden, Eric W.; Spurgeon on Revival; Zondervan; 1962

Hession, Roy; The Calvary Road; Christian Literature Crusade

Jewett, J. H.; The Passion for Souls; Revell; 1905

Kettner, Elmer A.; Adventures in Evangelism; Concordia; 1964

Kuiper, R. B.; God-Centered Evangelism; Baker; 1961

Latin American Mission Team; Evangelism-in-Depth; Moody; 1961

Little, P. E.; How to Give Away Your Faith; Inter-Varsity; 1966

Lockyer, Herbert; The Art of Winning Souls; Zondervan; 1954

Lovett, C. S.; Soul-Winning Is Easy; Zondervan; 1954

Lowry, Oscar; Scripture Memorizing for Successful Soul-Winning; Zondervan; 1962

McDormand, T. B.; The Christian Must Have the Answer; Broadman; 1969

Miller, Paul; Group Dynamics in Evangelism; Herald Press; 1958

Monsma, M. and others; Reformed Evangelism; Baker; 1948

Moore, W. B.; New Testament Follow-Up; Eerdmans; 1963

Mueller, Charles S.; The Strategy of Evangelism; Concordia; 1965

Munro, Harry C.; Fellowship-Evangelism Through Church Groups; Bethany Press, 1961

Murray, J., & Cummings, C.; Biblical Evangelism Today; Orthodox Presbyterian Church; 1954

Oates, Edward W.; Evangelism and Pastoral Psychology; (Pastoral Psychology VII, No. 65); 1956

Packer, J. I.; Evangelism and the Sovereignty of God; Inter-Varsity; 1961

Palmer, Kenyon A.; Kenyon Palmer's Scrapbook; Gideons International; 1952

Presbyterian Church in the U.S., Division of Evangelism; Workable Plan of Assimilation; Presbyterian Church in the U.S.

Presbyterian Church in the U.S., Inter-Agency Committee, General Council; Worship and Work of the Congregation; Presbyterian Church in the U.S.; 1963

Rees, Paul; Stir Up the Gift; Zondervan; 1952

Rinker, Rosalind; You Can Witness With Confidence; Zondervan; 1962

Sanny, Lorne; The Art of Personal Witnessing; Moody; 1957

Scarborough, L. R.; How Jesus Won Men; Doran; 1926

Shoemaker, S. M.; Revive Thy Church Beginning With Me; Harper and Row; 1948

Smith, Arthur J.; Without Excuse; Zondervan; 1964

Smith, O. J.; The Passion for Souls; Marshall, Morgan and Scott; 1952

Spurgeon, C. H.; The Soul-Winner; Eerdmans; 1963

Stott, John R. W.; Fundamentalism and Evangelism; Eerdmans; 1959

Stott, John R. W.; Our Guilty Silence; Eerdmans; 1969

Sweazey, Geo. F.; Effective Evangelism; Harper and Row; 1953

Terry, Mary; Winsome Witnessing; Moody; 1951

Trotman, Dawson E.; Born to Reproduce; The Navigators; 1955

Trotman, Dawson E.; Follow-Up; The Navigators; 1952

Trueblood, Elton; The Company of the Committed; Harper and Row; 1961

Trueblood, Elton; The Incendiary Fellowship; Harper and Row; 1967

Truett, George W.; A Quest for Souls, Sermons and Addresses; Eerdmans; 1917

Trumbull, Charles G.; Taking Men Alive; Revell; 1938

Walker, Alan; As Close As the Telephone; Abingdon; 1967

Warfield, Benjamin B.; The Plan of Salvation; Eerdmans; 1955

Weidman, Maurice; Christian Education and the Master Plan of Evangelism; National Sunday School Association; 1968

Whitesell, Faris; Basic New Testament Evangelism; Zondervan; 1949

Whitesell, Faris; Evangelistic Illustrations From the Bible; Zondervan

Whitesell, Faris; Great Personal Workers; Moody; 1956

Whitesell, Faris; Sixty-Five Ways to Give Evangelistic Invitations; Zondervan; 1945

Wilson, James J.; The Principles of War; Christian Books in Annapolis; 1964

Wilson, Walter; Remarkable New Stories Told by the Doctor; Moody; 1940

Wilson, Walter; Romance of a Doctor's Visits; Moody; 1936

Wilson, Walter; Strange Short Stories; Zondervan; 1936

Witty, Robert G.; Church Visitation; Broadman; 1967

Wolf, C. J. C.; Jonathan Edwards on Evangelism; Eerdmans; 1958

Wood, A. Skevington; Evangelism, Its Theology and Practice; Zondervan; 1966

Index

Notes

Notes

Notes

Assignments

Assignments

Assignments